D0909652

The Sixth Canon

Studies in Rhetoric/Communication
Thomas W. Benson, *Series Editor*

THE SIXTH CANON:

*Belletristic Rhetorical Theory
and Its French Antecedents*

Barbara Warnick

University of South Carolina Press

P301.3
.G7
W37
1993

Copyright © 1993 University of South Carolina

Published in Columbia, South Carolina, by the
University of South Carolina Press

Manufactured in the United States of America

Library of Congress Cataloging-in-Publication Data

Warnick, Barbara, 1946–
    The sixth canon : belletristic rhetorical theory and its French
antecedents / Barbara Warnick.
        p.   cm. — (Studies in rhetoric/communication)
    Includes bibliographical references (p.) and index.
    ISBN 0–87249–892–1
    1. Rhetoric—Great Britain—History.   2. Rhetoric—France—
History.   3. Rhetoric—1500–1800.   4. Aesthetics, French.
5. Rhetoric and psychology.   6. Communication—Philosophy.
I. Title.   II. Series.
P301.3.G7W37   1993
808′.00941—dc20   93–20266

To Michael

APR 1 6 1998

Nothing is more capable of infusing any passion into the mind, than eloquence, by which objects are represented in the strongest and most lively colours.

David Hume, *Four Dissertations*

Contents

Foreword

This book is of major importance to studies of the history of rhetoric—indeed to the history of modern Western thought. Professor Warnick's presentation significantly reinterprets eighteenth- and nineteenth-century theories of rhetoric and rhetorical instruction. Her book specifies the intellectual forces that generated the "new," allegedly "managerial," rhetorical theories of the eighteenth and nineteenth centuries.

The influence of French philosophical and literary thought on eighteenth-century British ideas about human communication has long been recognized, but how the French theories were integrated and modified by "enlightenment" Scots has not until now been thoroughly explored. Cartesian influences in France have been re-explored, but Warnick goes on to show just how in their theories of verbal creativity French theorists and pedagogues replaced concepts of the "rational" with such aesthetic considerations as the roles of portraiture, nature, taste, propriety, imagination, intuition, and "the Sublime." She shows further how leading eighteenth-century Scottish rhetoricians assimilated these notions and gave them psycho-physiological explanations, thereby promulgating a "new rhetoric" undergirded by a new psychological/aesthetic theory of communication and instantiating a "sixth canon" of rhetorical invention and criticism.

In this century it has been customary to associate seventeenth- and eighteenth-century alterations in rhetorical theory and criticism almost exclusively with the emergence of modern science and scientific method. Warnick makes clear that revisionary French and other notions of aesthetics were at least equally influential in the shift. These deeply influenced even the scientifically oriented Scottish rhetoricians. She also shows how the relatively recent contention that the resulting, "new," eighteenth-century British rhetoric was "managerial," in the sense of embodying no concern with processes of rhetorical invention, oversimplifies. Often drawing on the French, Scottish rhetoricians did indeed set logical considerations outside their conceptions of rhetorical invention and form, but they substituted psychologized conceptions of aesthetic creativity and response and thereby created a "sixth rhetorical canon." Warnick shows clearly, for the first time, that the "new" British rhetoric of the eighteenth century was in fact an integration of French aesthetic and British psychological premises.

Carroll C. Arnold

Preface

I became interested in this project for two reasons. First, I noticed frequent citations by Scottish belletrists Adam Smith, George Campbell, and Hugh Blair of seventeenth-century French rhetorics, and I also noted that these Scottish rhetoricians used the same examples and passages that their French predecessors had used as illustrations. Second, I recognized that there was a noticeable lack of interest by these French and Scottish authors in what has traditionally been called the canon of invention. The belletrist framework seemed to have transformed the agenda of neoclassical Renaissance rhetorics into something entirely different. Instead of concern about invention and the production of discourse, belletristic rhetorics appeared to be pervasively fascinated with aesthetics and the development of receptive competence. This book examines this belletrist transformation of rhetoric, and in particular its French antecedents.

This study has drawn upon a wide range of editions and translations of seventeenth- and eighteenth-century works. In citing these authors, I have endeavored to preserve the flavor of the original texts while making them accessible to the modern reader. At times, this has meant retaining the masculine pronoun reference, as well as archaic spellings of both French and English words as they appeared in the original editions. When modern editions or translations were available, I have used them. If no standard translation of a French text was available, I have translated it myself. Hopefully, the dual note system, which places the original French citation at the bottom of the page, will assist the reader in following the text while keeping in view an author's thought as originally expressed.

Without the generosity and support of my colleagues, this project would not have been possible. I would like to acknowledge a release-time grant provided to me by the College of Arts and Sciences of the University of Washington which enabled me to complete my study of the Bolevian Sublime which appears in chapter 3 of this book. I would also like to acknowledge *Rhetorica* and its editor Michael Leff who granted me permission to use in chapter 3 large portions of my essay "The Bolevian Sublime in Eighteenth-Century British Rhetorical Theory," *Rhetorica* 4 (1990), 349–69. I would also like to thank Lawrence Bliquez of the University of Washington Classics Department who assisted me with technical problems related to work on chapter 3. Furthermore, I want to note the absolutely first-rate assistance of Jon Bouknight, who served as my research assistant during the time I was writing chapter 4.

The person who originally suggested considering the question of "what became of invention in the modern period?" was Carroll Arnold. Not only did he generate the original idea for this study, he carefully nursed it along through three revisions. Carroll is, as another author in this series has noted, an "editor's editor." Those of use who have had the privilege of working with him have learned a great deal. Finally, I would like to thank Thomas M. Carr, Jr. and Vincent Bevilacqua who served as external reviewers for the Press and who suggested final refinements and improvements in the manuscript.

The Sixth Canon

Introduction

In 1748, Adam Smith began a series of public lectures in
Edinburgh on rhetoric and belles lettres.[1] Intended by their or-
ganizers to broaden the education of budding lawyers, Smith's
lectures soon attracted the leading literati, lawyers, and other
gentlemen of Edinburgh and were continued for two more
years until Smith left to assume a post at Glasgow University.[2]
Smith's lectures, which dealt with the history of language,
forms of expression, virtues of style, and various discursive
genres (descriptive, narrative, poetic, and oratorical), bore little
resemblance to more traditional rhetorics. Smith seemed much
more concerned to provide an account of correct language use,
the qualities of a good prose style, the varieties of emotion and
means of expressing them, and the means of attaining solid
comprehension by one's audience than he was to address many
of the more traditional concerns, such as how to invent arguments or establish the credibility of the speaker.

In his sixth lecture, Smith disparaged detailed treatment
of tropes and figures. Of invention and argument, he likewise
had little to say: "I might now . . . proceed to point out the
proper method of choosing the arguments and the manner of
arranging them as well as the Expression. But Directions of
this sort can seldom be of any advantage. The arguments that
are to be used before a people cannot be very intricate; the
Proposition generally requires no Proof at all and when it does
the arguments are of themselves so evident as not to require
any elaborate explanation. . . . As the arguments are in themselves so simple, there can be no great nicety required in the
arrangement."[3]

Inventio, one of the five canons of classical rhetoric, was
thus passed over in Smith's lectures. Instead of focusing on the
persuasive strategies a speaker might use to influence an au-

1

dience in legal, demonstrative, or deliberative speaking, Smith emphasized perspicuity and propriety of expression. For him the chief virtue of discourse was to so express oneself that the idea or passion conveyed could be readily and fully experienced by the auditor or reader. Or, as Smith himself put it, "when the sentiment of a speaker is expressed in a neat, clear, plain and clever manner, and the passion or affection he is possessed of and intends, *by sympathy* to communicate to his hearer, is plainly and cleverly hit off, then and then only the expression has all the force and beauty that language can give it."[4] Smith's view was that the aim of all discourse was to be so cast up that the experience it conveys is readily replicated in the experience of the hearer or reader. As an intellective (as opposed to pathetic) criterion for judging discourse, this requirement was assimilated into "propriety" which implied, as Brian Vickers has said, "that the listener will judge the speaker's accuracy in expressing emotion by reference to what he has himself felt on similar occasions."[5] Propriety in narration meant that events should be ordered as experience dictates. Its presence in drama was judged by whether characters were portrayed so as to conform with their stations and ideal types, and in description by whether various elements were naturally interconnected. Such principles formed the core of Smith's theory of discourse; they also provided the linchpin of belletristic rhetorics that were to follow Smith's.

Blair and the Transition to Belletrism

One of the attendees at Smith's lectures was the young Hugh Blair who was later appointed Regius Professor of Rhetoric and Belles Lettres at the University of Edinburgh and who served in that capacity for twenty-one years.[6] Whereas Smith's lectures were never published (he ordered them destroyed prior to his death), Blair did publish his in 1783.[7] Translated into French, Italian, Russian, and Spanish, Blair's lectures were subsequently issued in twenty-six editions in Great Britain and thirty-seven in the United States.[8]

To a considerable degree, it is Blair's work that is considered most representative of belletrism during the Scottish enlightenment.[9] His lectures displayed all of the major features of belletrism and exemplified the phenomenon. Blair had two purposes in mind in addressing his student audience. The first was to improve their skill in composition and speaking. The second was "to improve their taste with respect to writing and discourse" by laying out the principles that would "enable them to judge for themselves in that part of literature called the Belles Lettres."[10] Blair's means of improving the skill and taste of his auditors were the same as Smith's. In treating the various discursive genres—eloquence, historical writing, poetry, tragedy, and comedy—Blair would define or demarcate the genre, identify desirable and undesirable elements, then comment on signal examples drawn from historical and contemporary texts. As lecturer, then, Blair served as a model critic. His role was to exemplify the proper responses to eloquence and literature. If he succeeded, his students could themselves learn the proper means of responding to texts and thus qualify for life in cultured Scottish society. They could acquire taste, in short.

The belletrist rhetorics of Smith and Blair were quite different, then, from the rhetorics of such neoclassicists as John Ward and John Lawson.[11] Ward and Lawson carried forward the Aristotelian concern for production and strategic influence via the artistic modes of proof—*ethos, pathos,* and *logos.* Viewing themselves as providing advice to the orator, these neoclassicists counselled readers on the forms and modes of proof, the arrangement of arguments, levels of style, and the selection and application of various figures and tropes. Ward and Lawson coached their readers on how to construct a good speech, while Smith and Blair demonstrated the proper responses to the varieties and virtues of all forms of discourse. Nancy Struever has emphasized the particular nature of these eighteenth-century theories:

> The practical nature of the eighteenth-century program . . . both shapes intellectual discipline and invests social behavior. The ability to engage in pleasant and informal, "polite" argument and in the argumentative development of moral and aesthetic judgment, "taste," constitutes a general receptive competence. . . . Rhetorical discipline is reassembled as a new skill which is the duty, property,

and talent of a new social elite; the faculties to be developed in education and social intercourse enhance, give meaning to, status and connection: taste, for example, is a mode of social communication, the hegemonous social competence.[12]

The development of receptive competence was a principal aim of the belletrists; it shaped and profoundly influenced their agendas and their methods. It was to this end that they compared languages as to harmony, perspicuity, and flexibility; provided critical commentary on the authors of their day; and articulated criteria applicable to each of the genres of discourse. Smith and Blair did not entirely neglect their listeners' concerns about composition and speaking by any means. They provided general advice on how to write well, how to order events and materials, how to deliver speeches, and other matters of productive competence. But in their works the concern with production is matched if not overridden by a concern for receptive acumen.

Scottish Belletrists and "The Sixth Canon"

Belletrist rhetorics and studies of belles lettres were particularly concerned with examining the specific qualities of discourse and their effects. This pattern was clearly reflected in the headings for Blair's lectures: "Taste," "Criticism—Genius—Pleasures of Taste—Sublimity in Objects," "The Sublime in Writing," "Beauty, and other Pleasures of Taste." To some extent, an agenda such as this was influenced by Francis Hutcheson who had held that, parallel to the external senses (sight, taste, touch, etc.) there were internal senses: "the author chooses to call . . . our Power of perceiving the Beauty of Regularity, Order, Harmony, an Internal Sense. . . ."[13] Working from this internal reflex sense theory of reception, Smith and Blair, along with George Campbell, sought to delineate and clarify aesthetic discursive qualities that affected listeners and readers.[14] As Walter John Hipple has noted, in eighteenth-century British aesthetics, problems were to be stated and solved in terms of simple and elementary ideas and feelings, "there are certain particular feelings, the sentiments of beauty (or of sublimity, or picturesqueness, or of the ridiculous) which require careful discrimination; then they must be accounted for. . . . What were the circumstances of natural or artificial things which evoke these particular sentiments? And by what mechanism do they do so? In all, three problems: distinguishing the feelings themselves, isolating causal circumstances, and discovering the mechanisms of causation."[15]

As Hipple went on to observe, rhetoric, because of its long history of distinguishing genres and qualities of discourse and considering psychological response to them, was a particularly fertile field for considering this aesthetic sense. Therefore, the aesthetic dimensions of various qualities of discourse preoccupied Smith, Campbell, and Blair. The purpose of this book is to consider three critical senses thematized in their works—propriety, sublimity, and taste. Propriety represented the intellective domain of aesthetic influence. Believing as they did that discourse was a reflection of the experience of its receivers, the belletrists sought to identify the particular dimensions (chronology, style, depiction, arrangement) along which discourse could be experienced as proportionate and suitable and thus plausible and aesthetically satisfying. The Sublime represented the pathetic dimension of aesthetic influence. When encountering the Sublime, the mind was said to enlarge itself with awe and admiration and to respond involuntarily and naturally. The belletrists took care to dissociate this Sublime from strategic use of style and to invest it as a touchstone of creativity, grandeur, and uniqueness.

Whereas propriety and sublimity were qualities of discourse itself, taste was viewed as a capacity of the recipient. As has been noted, taste was indeed the catalyst for a good deal of critical activity. It had its analog in the predispositions and cognitive beliefs of audiences in Aristotelian theory, and the belletrists were concerned about describing the nature and workings of taste. Their writings displayed an empiricist tendency to equate taste with sensory capacity and a common-sense impulse to stress the importance of cognition and judgment in taste. All of the belletrists agreed, too, that there was an elite somewhere to which one could look to establish a taste standard.

To fulfill their role as model critics and to develop the receptive capabilities and taste of their students and readers, Smith, Blair, and Campbell set about "conceptualizing" propriety, sublimity, taste, and other dimensions of reception. In this process, these concepts emerged into consciousness as distinct entities and were defined, exemplified, and taught to students as topics of interest.[16] That is to say, the belletrists identified these senses, described their empirical affects and constituents, and thereby showed how the aesthetic appeal of a discourse was essential to its rhetorical effect. This conceptualization of propriety, sublimity, and taste will be the focus of this book. In its course, I intend to establish this corpus of work as a "sixth canon" of rhetoric, an amalgam of aesthetics and psychology that arose in the seventeenth and eighteenth centuries and that supplanted standard treatments of invention and its commonplaces as contained in neoclassical rhetorics. Further, I will argue that we cannot fully understand the emergence and nature of this sixth canon unless we consider its antecedents in the works of the seventeenth-century French belletrists who preceded the Scots.

French Belletrism

That there was a French belletrism preceding the Scots' is a well known fact, but the nature of that phenomenon and its influence on Scottish rhetorics has not yet been examined.[17] French rhetorics having belletristic attributes included René Rapin's *Comparaisons des grands hommes de l'antiquité* and his *Réflexions sur l'éloquence* (1684), Bernard Lamy's *L'Art de parler* (1676), François Fénelon's *Dialogues sur l'éloquence* (1718) and his *Lettre à l'Académie* (1716), and Charles Rollin's *De la manière d'enseigner et d'étudier les belles lettres* (1726–28).[18] These works shared significant characteristics with the Scottish rhetorics of Smith, Blair, and Campbell. They modeled the critical impulse, sought to develop taste in their readers, focused on aesthetic dimensions of discourse, and treated the various genres of speaking and writing together as an ensemble. All of these works were rhetorics or contained sections that explained how to communicate effectively with an audience, and they all put forward models from the eloquence of ancient and contemporary speakers.

In addition to these rhetorics, certain other French works
will be included here because they were widely read and frequently cited by the Scottish belletrists and because they
treated topics and issues relevant to "the sixth canon." Dominique Bouhours' *Entretiens d'Ariste et d'Eugène* (1683) and *La
Manière de bien penser dans les ouvrages d'esprit* (1687) used
threaded-together excerpts from the works of ancient and modern authors to illustrate judgments of good taste and good
sense.[19] Expressed in dialogue form, Bouhours' works were intended to illustrate the conversations of the salons where taste
was developed and displayed through comparisons among authors and a savoring of the *bon mot*. Nicolas Boileau-Despréaux
contributed to eighteenth-century literary theory through his
L'Art poétique which articulated neoclassical standards for poetry and drama and his translation of "Longinus' " *On the Sublime*.[20] Both of Boileau's works appeared in 1674, and while the
former was cited only sporadically during the Scottish Enlightenment, the latter provided the catalyst for a major *topos* of
criticism throughout the eighteenth century. Finally, the Scottish rhetorics drew liberally from Jean-Baptiste Dubos' *Réflexions critiques sur la poésie et sur la peinture* (1719).[21] This work
drew together impressionistic conclusions from aesthetic
speculations of Dubos' day and insisted upon effect as the standard by which works of art and poetry were to be judged. Dubos' method was empirical and subjectivist, and his effort to
establish introspection as the specific principle of aesthetics
was attractive to later theorists who subscribed to associationist psychology.[22]

Despite the striking similarities between them, French and
Scottish belletrism were separated by profound differences.
The works of Rapin, Fénelon, Boileau, and Lamy were produced in an age of rationalism. Even though only Lamy among
these four was explicitly influenced by Descartes, the others
pursued the neoclassical aim of discovering a stable aesthetic
standard by which all works could be judged. For example, Boileau's *Art poétique* set the guidelines for poetic genres, while
his work on the Sublime endeavored to establish that concept
as an overarching critical touchstone. The British empiricists,
on the other hand, had a very different aim. They began by
contemplating actual experience and from that derived ac-

counts of the works of the human mind and human nature. In Smith's view, rhetoric was justified as a field of study in part because "the best method of explaining and illustrating the various powers of the human mind, the most useful part of metaphysics, arises from an examination of the several ways of communicating our thoughts by speech, and from an attention to the principles of those literary compositions which contribute to persuasion or entertainment. By these arts, everything that we perceive or feel, every operation of our minds is expressed and delineated in such a manner, that it may be clearly distinguished and remembered."[23] The contrast between the rationalist and empiricist perspectives is nowhere more clear than in the French and Scots' respective treatments of the Sublime. For the French neoclassicists, the Sublime provided a standard against which the aesthetic qualities of a discourse could be measured. For the Scots, the Sublime was one dimension of discourse among others (e.g., the novel, the beautiful, the picturesque) which inspired responses of a certain kind in the recipient. This contrast and its implications for rhetoric will be fully explored in chapter 3 of this book.

A second significant difference between the French and Scottish belletrists was the psychological theory that undergirded their views of rhetoric. In France, Descartes' view of the mind's workings was widely held. In brief, Descartes believed that emotions and passions were aroused when external stimuli caused vibrations in the nerves, and these were transmitted to the brain by the blood's animal spirits.[24] This meant that the capacities for artistic production and aesthetic response were tightly related to a person's physiological makeup. For example, Dubos claimed that "the genius of [the] Arts consists in a happy arrangement of the brain's organs, in the good structure of each of these organs as in the quality of the blood, which disposes it to ferment during work in such a way that it furnishes an abundance of spirits to the springs which serve the function of the imagination."[25/a] The effect of a view such as

---

a. le genie [des] Arts consiste en un arrangement heureux des organes du cerveau, dans la bonne conformation de chacun de ces organes, comme dans la qualité du sang, laquelle le dispose à fermenter durant le travail, de maniere qu'il fournisse en abondance des esprits aux ressorts qui servent aux fonctions de l'imagination.

this was to reduce influence and aesthetic response to a sort of mechanical process. As Jean-Paul Sermain observed, "the complex routes of the animal spirits, this come-and-go between the senses and the mind, the heart and the imagination, serve as a scientific alibi for the assimilation of discourse to a machine. . . ."[26/b]

The Scottish belletrists' account of the mind's workings arose from the experimental and/or empirical orientations of Francis Bacon, John Locke, and David Hume.[27] Their view, which originated in faculty psychology and folded in principles of association, was made most explicit in George Campbell's *The Philosophy of Rhetoric*. The mind was viewed essentially as passive, constructing knowledge through assimilation of experiences of concrete particular objects. Mental contents were comprised of sensations (internal states or experience of external qualities), memory (prints left by sensible impressions), and imagination (all other ideas as composites of sensations and memory). The mind was said to assemble or combine ideas through patterns of association such as resemblance, contiguity, and causation. Rhetoric thus worked by appealing to the imagination. Rhetoric simulated sensations by making ideas lively and vivid, thus transferring energy from an already lively idea to a languid one.[28] Campbell believed that ideas were made lively or vivid through representation and resemblance: "the imagination is addressed by exhibiting to it a lively and beautiful representation of a suitable object. As in this exhibition, the task of the orator may, in some sort, be said, like that of the painter, to consist in imitation. . . ."[29] The orator's task, then was to make general ideas concrete, lively, and vivid—to represent them, as it were.

Thus, one of these theories of psychology extrapolated an account of the mind's workings from supposed physiological processes. The other began with individual experience and universalized it to an account of human nature. As far as rhetoric was concerned, the effect was the same, because both Cartesian and empiricist psychologies de-emphasized cognition and

---

b. Les parcours complexes des esprits animaux, ce va-et-vient entre les sens et l'esprit, le coeur et l'imagination, servent d'alibi scientifique à l'assimilation du discours à une machine. . . .

instead insisted upon the importance of sensory stimulation in generating affective response. Speaking and writing were viewed as successful to the extent that they painted experience and made it sensible. Thus, and very importantly, aesthetic criteria such as propriety and clarity received the attention formerly given to processes of reasoning and logic.

The Sixth Canon as a "Rhetorical Theory"

The attenuation and near disappearance of invention and its replacement by aesthetic/psychological accounts of rhetorical affect have been well recognized by scholars of eighteenth-century British rhetorical theories. The shift away from interest in artistic "rational" proofs was noted by Douglas Ehninger who observed that classical concern for commonplaces and stasis theory arose from a generalized orientation toward the speech element of the speaker/speech/hearer triad. Eighteenth-century Scottish empiricists were much more preoccupied with the hearer, with investigating the principles of the mind by which hearers were led to understand and believe what they heard. Consequently, "the classical notion of *inventio* as a technique of search and discovery gives way to a more comprehensive concept, and that familiar eighteenth-century doctrine of the 'management' or 'conduct' of a discourse is born. . . . The selection of arguments, the evaluation of their strength, the determination of the manner in which they may most tellingly be presented—these and many other considerations become inventional problems. The whole rationale of the old order is swept away, and the classical distribution of functions among the various departments of rhetoric is irretrievably lost."[30]

Ehninger's emphasis on a managerial rather than generative or epistemic view of rational proof in belletristic rhetorics has since been widely accepted by other scholars.[31] Its implications were partially noted by James L. Golden and Edward P. J. Corbett: "By eliminating the role of discovery from *inventio* Campbell [and] Blair . . . altered the starting point to be used in speech preparation. Speakers can assume that since arguments and proof are present from the outset, their principal challenge is to learn how to manage rather than invent or discover ideas."[32] The result of all this, of course, was that the classical canons of *inventio* and *dispositio* became blurred.

Recognition of the absence of traditional inventional theory in the works of Smith, Blair, and Campbell has not been accompanied by a commensurate appreciation of the importance of aesthetic appeal in their theories. It would be hard to ignore the Scottish authors' preoccupation with the Sublime, beauty, novelty, propriety, and the like, but few commentators have seen that this preoccupation replaced notions comparable to traditional theories of invention. For example, after noting Campbell's preoccupation with perspicuity and vivacity as the means of enlivening ideas, Lloyd Bitzer went on to argue: "It is worth noting that although Campbell mentions aesthetic qualities of style . . . by virtue of which rhetoric is a fine art, he treats style as exclusively functional. He interprets style not as an appendage to communication but as the indispensable agency of effective communication; he interprets techniques of style not as ornaments but as means of enlivening ideas."[33] In noting the significance of concreteness and specificity in Campbell's theory, his insistence on using the sensible to represent the intelligible, the individual to represent the genus, and the animate for the inanimate, Bitzer hinted at the nature of the sixth canon's workings. Unfortunately, he devoted only brief attention to such matters and focused instead on his central purpose, which was to demonstrate the influence of Hume on Campbell's *The Philosophy of Rhetoric*.

Wilbur Samuel Howell lamented that "too often, alas, the rhetorical works of Blair and his contemporaries have been studied as if their sole rhetorical content abides at those points where they are obviously close to the old rhetoric of Aristotle and Cicero."[34] Howell's statement here is quite applicable to his own work when it comes to the sixth canon. In his *Eighteenth-Century British Logic and Rhetoric*, Howell treated the belletristic rhetoricians according to a specific agenda. He wanted to determine where each of them stood on six issues separating the "old" rhetoric from the "new"—whether their works focused on persuasive discourse only or on a broader group of genres, whether they limited themselves to formal artistic proofs, whether their reasoning forms were inductive or deductive, whether they dealt in probabilities or scientific standards of proof, whether they made use of preset organizational forms, and whether they endorsed a plain or a figured style.[35] Since these distinctions grew out of traditional conceptions of logic, disposition, and style, Howell left little room for noticing the role of aesthetics. He was thus predisposed to summarize the works and comment upon the extent to which they departed from tradition on the six issues but was not moved to explore the implications of the Scots' interest in the aesthetic dimensions of discourse. In Howell's 700-page study, there is one index citation to sublimity and one to beauty.[36] In his study of eighteenth-century logic and rhetoric, Howell does allude to Blair's views on taste and Campbell's on vivacity, but his consideration of the aesthetic dimension of rhetorical appeal is always very much in passing.

Elsewhere, however, Howell made a fine contribution on this topic. His study of the relation of poetry to oratory in Fénelon's works illuminated the role of portraiture and propriety in Fénelon's conception of rhetoric. In Howell's view, Fénelon's originality arose from his awareness that pleasure was an essential intermediate means of persuading and that vivid representation was an undeniably effective means of capturing the imagination and attention of auditors. Howell then concluded that Fénelon was "here suggesting the impossibility of divorcing expression from communication or aesthetics from logic. . . . He sees no point in treating [aesthetic] response as if one could unerringly separate its pleasurable from its intellectual phases."[37] More will be said of Fénelon's emphasis on portraiture in chapter 2 of this study.

A good example of the ways that a five-canon model can impair scholarly study of belles lettres can be found in the dissertation of one of the finest scholars of the period—Vincent Bevilacqua. Completed in 1961 at the University of Illinois, Bevilacqua's dissertation on the rhetorical theory of Henry Home, Lord Kames, was comprised of seven chapters: an introduction, a study of Kames' life, a chapter on each of the five canons, and a conclusion. Some of the chapters were rather short, since Kames was not a rhetorician and did not produce a rhetoric. Bevilacqua began his chapter on *inventio* by noting that Kames had "no systematic theory of invention" and that consideration of that topic must be derived from "a patchwork of scattered remarks and observations incidental to more immediate concerns."[38] Bevilacqua concluded the chapter by observing that "Kames' inventio . . . is concerned with the structure and efficiency of logical and psychological arguments and with their origins in human nature; it is not concerned with finding out what to say or with the invention of arguments."[39] By 1963, Bevilacqua had completely discarded the five-canon approach to Kames and was led to argue that "since in his writings he does not view rhetoric as composed of the five arts of invention, arrangement, style, memory, and delivery, his theory of rhetoric is not traditional or Ciceronian."[40]

In subsequent work, Bevilacqua has contributed more than any other scholar to an understanding of the aesthetic dimension of belletristic rhetorical theories. In a 1963 study of Kames, Bevilacqua noted Kames' effort to ascertain the origin and function of such qualities as grandeur, sublimity, novelty, uniformity, variety, and propriety, as well as Kames' belief that principles of effective communication should accord with the common sense and faculties of human nature. Noting Kames' interest in psychological predispositions and propensities, Bevilacqua articulated certain Kamesian principles of communication: that a style's naturalness and efficacy grew out of the degree of consonance between thought and expression; that discourse should be so ordered as to reflect proportionately the order and nature of that to which it referred; and that clarity and avoidance of obscurity were preeminent qualities of style.[41] These principles were derived from the conviction that the discourse which best suits the mental habits, predispositions, and propensities of an audience will be most effective; this point of view formed the basis for the union of aesthetics and rhetoric in belletristic theories. Bevilacqua's later studies on Campbell and Blair have taken these theorists on their own terms and delineated the philosophical origins of their theories. In the case of Campbell, Bevilacqua explored the doctrine of sympathy as the foundation for a new theory of *ethos,* and he reexamined the dimensions of vivacity, in particular its connection to the Sublime and its use of uncommon resemblances.[42] In regard to Blair, Bevilacqua emphasized the importance of the "internal reflex sense" theory drawn from Francis Hutcheson. who considered aesthetic response as immediate, involuntary, and essentially noncognitive in nature.[43]

Bevilacqua concluded his study of Campbell by saying that "critics have given but little attention [to] the influence of prevailing moral and aesthetic theory. The oversight is serious, for [Campbell] . . . frequently applied the assumption that such moral and aesthetic principles as sympathy, novelty, beauty, and sublimity have rhetorical implications."[44] Although Bevilacqua has taken us some distance in considering the aesthetic dimension of belletristic rhetorics, further work is needed, particularly because he did not include French authors in his study of the sixth canon. This neglect is all the more serious because it is precisely in the area of aesthetic influence that the French authors had the greatest influence on the Scots. As Dennis R. Bormann has noted, the French influence on works in eighteenth-century British rhetorical and aesthetic theory has been profound. Bormann advised scholars studying Campbell to consider the French influence if they would understand the intellectual milieu in which Campbell worked.[45] I believe that the same is true of Blair and of Smith, and that the influence of French belletrism on its Scottish successors must be systematically considered.

The French Influence

Near the end of his treatise on rhetoric, Campbell considered the many linguistic practices adopted by the British due to French influence: "The genuine source of most of these modern refinements is, in my opinion, an excessive bias to everything that bears a resemblance to what is found in France. . . . I own that this may happen insensibly, without design or affectation on the part of our writers; and that either from the close intercourse which we have with that nation, or from the great use that we make of their writings, and the practice now so frequent of translating them"[46] Among the literati and gentlemen of Scottish society, knowledge of French language and literature was a sine qua non of cultured life. Keith Marshall has noted that while French was not an official part of the educational syllabus until the nineteenth century, "at least a reading knowledge of French was a necessary part of the accomplishments of a gentleman, it was taught unofficially all around the universities by mid century, in a number of the grammar schools and privately."[47]

All of the French belletristic rhetorics were available in English translation by the middle of the eighteenth century; Lamy's *Art of Speaking* appeared in 1676, Rapin's *Critical Works* in 1706, Fénelon's *Letter* and his *Dialogues* in 1722, Rollin's *Method of Teaching and Studying the Belles Lettres* in 1734, and Dubos' *Critical Reflections* in 1748.[48] While the existence of these translations indicates widespread British interest in continental works, it is somewhat immaterial to French belletrism's influence on the Scots literati. Smith, Blair, and Campbell all read French works in the original language.

Smith, for example, was an excellent scholar in both classical and modern languages. D. D. Raphael has reported that at Balliol College, Oxford, "Smith read a wide range of Greek and Latin literature. . . . He also read a fair amount of French literature and took pleasure in translating memorable passages into English."[49] Smith's *Lectures on Rhetoric and Belles Lettres* apparently cited Rousseau, Balzac, Dubos, Rapin, Fléchier, and Descartes, among others.[50] Close study of French influences on Smith is rendered impossible by the absence of a manuscript text of the *Lectures*. The student copyists who recorded Smith's lectures were apparently not conversant in French, since they regularly left blanks where French names should have been recorded, or misspelled the names.[51] I shall therefore consider only Smith's conception of propriety which was very likely influenced by French conceptions of *bienséance* and *vraisemblance* and which was so central for Smith.

Having studied humanities, Greek, logic, and natural philosophy for nine years at the University of Edinburgh, Blair surely read French.[52] Of one hundred twenty-five citations of French authors in Blair's lectures, twenty were clearly from works cited in French.[53] Blair's use of Rollin, Crévier, and Fénelon will be discussed in chapter 2 of this work, and his reliance upon Boileau's theory of the Sublime will be considered in chapter 3. In his *Lectures,* Blair's extensive use of French critical theories and literature made his awareness and admiration for continental works everywhere apparent.

Campbell's writings on grammatical purity, perspicuity,

word choice, arrangement, and other matters depended heavily on comparisons among languages to illustrate the principles of correct usage. The two languages most frequently compared were French and English. Campbell believed the French language was unnecessarily redundant and ambiguous in pronoun use, word references, elisions, and contractions, and he called upon his thorough knowledge of French to illustrate these problems.[54] In regard to the sixth canon, Campbell made use of Boileau's conception of the Sublime, Dubos' rationale for the attractiveness of lively ideas, Fénelon's views on artistic unobtrusiveness, and Rollin's theories of style.[55] On the whole, Campbell cited over a dozen French authors, and all citations to specific works were to untranslated editions. Furthermore, Campbell's account of the distinction between probability and plausibility drew heavily from the French conception of *vraisemblance,* and Campbell explicitly acknowledged his indebtedness on this point.[56]

To trace the nature and extent of French belletrism's influence upon the Scots and upon their conceptions of the aesthetic dimension of rhetoric, I shall move geographically from the continent toward Britain and chronologically from the late seventeenth to the late eighteenth century. Chapter 1 begins with Lamy's *L'Art de parler,* the first "modern" rhetoric to cast aside the trappings of traditional rhetorics and produce a theory of persuasion grounded in Cartesian psychology. This chapter will establish the senses in which Lamy and his successors, Bouhours, Fénelon, Rollin, and Dubos, viewed adjustment of discourse to an audience's culture, predispositions, and habits of mind as essential to rhetorical success. Chapter 2 will consider the connection of propriety to social practices in the *ancien régime,* as well as the importance of harmony, coherence, and proportion in Fénelon's aesthetics. Noting the conversion of propriety into sympathy in Smith's rhetoric, the chapter will examine how propriety was interpreted in Smith's and Blair's rhetorics.

The Sublime as a quality of discourse and art was presumed by the rhetoricians of the Scottish Enlightenment to be perceptible to the man of taste. It thus functioned as the barometer of a person's ability to judge and discern excellence in discourse. Blair and others treated it, along with beauty, by attempting to discern its nature and the characteristics of its identification. Chapter 3 will consider the Sublime as it originated in Boileau's translation of the pseudo-Longinian *On the Sublime*. Blair's conception of the Sublime was wholly derived from Boileau's, whereas the materialist or "scientific" conception of the Sublime put forward by Joseph Priestley owed very little to the French theorist. The fortunes and malleability of the Bolevian Sublime in eighteenth-century rhetorics illustrate what can become of a concept when it is removed from its original context and set down in works whose agenda departs considerably from the original.

Aristotle had considered rhetoric to be a general, overarching productive art, the "faculty of discovering the possible means of persuasion in reference to any subject whatsoever."[57] Noting that this was the function of no other art, he emphasized its generality, its concern with persuasion in reference to any given subject. In Enlightenment rhetorics such as those of Smith, Blair, Campbell and their French predecessors, there was a receptive faculty corresponding to the productive faculty of persuasion, and that faculty was taste. The person possessing taste could distinguish works of artistic merit from shams and could explain why by considering such qualities as propriety and sublimity. Most theorists agreed that like a taste for wine or for good food, the taste for art was a natural capacity that could be cultivated and enhanced through experience, but they disagreed on issues concerning the role of cognition in taste and the nature of variability in taste. The many controversies between empiricists and commonsense theorists concerning taste, the overarching receptive faculty, will be the subject of chapter 4 of this book, which will conclude with consideration of a particular French theory of taste that influenced many of the aestheticians of the Scottish Enlightenment.

The topic of taste will illustrate how the problem of receptive competence became the site of conflicts between classicism and scientism, rationalism and empiricism, and skepticism and commonsense philosophy. What one discovers when examining the belletristic rhetorics of the Scots literati is that each of them is a fabric woven from diverse intellectual threads in various proportions.

Chapter 1

Lamy's *L'Art de parler* and the Eclipse of Invention

Balthasar Gibert was a traditionalist. A teacher of rhetoric at the University of Paris' Collège de Mazarin, Gibert prided himself on over forty years of classroom experience teaching fifteen-year-old students the rudiments of rhetoric. The foundation and substance of Gibert's course were drawn from classical lore—Aristotle, Hermagoras, Cicero, and Quintilian. In Gibert's classroom, students studied the concepts and precepts generated by these authors, composed writing assignments based on standard, universal propositions, and memorized the basic terms and definitions of the classical canon. Gibert insisted that this was the only way to study rhetoric, and in his *La Rhétorique, ou les règles de l'éloquence* (1730) he argued "we thus do not promise to give here rules that no one has yet given: on the contrary, we pride ourselves on following, in this matter, only in the footsteps of the Ancients."[1/a]

Gibert established a distinguished career as a rhetorical pedagogue and author. In 1703, he published his *Traité de la véritable éloquence,* followed over a decade later by the *Jugements des savants sur les auteurs qui ont traité de la rhétorique.*[2] He steadfastly criticized individuals such as Charles Rollin and Bernard Lamy who sought to modernize rhetoric and align it with post-Cartesian and Enlightenment world views. Rollin received Gibert's disapproval for advocating rhetorical instruction in the vernacular and for using examples from modern authors in his *Traité des études.*[3] Lamy's rhetoric was condemned by Gibert because of its adoption of geometrical proofs, its incomplete treatment of the passions and of style, and its failure to provide explicit precepts for rhetorical prac-

---

a. Nous ne promettons donc pas de donner ici des Regles que personne n'ait encore données: au contraire, nous faisons gloire de ne suivre, en cette matiere, que les traces des Anciens.

18

tice.[4] Gibert was indeed the French equivalent of John Ward and John Lawson. His rhetorical theory was avowedly neoclassical, and if one seeks an impression of the tradition to which modern rhetorics of the late seventeenth and early eighteenth centuries were reacting, one can get a clear picture of the neoclassicism of that period by examining Gibert's works.

Gibert's *Règles de l'éloquence* was intended as a resource manual for teachers of rhetoric. It was organized according to the first three of the five rhetorical canons—invention, disposition, and style. The section on invention provided readers with suggestions on how to help their students find, select, arrange, and treat various proofs. It also contained extensive advice on how to amplify a composition. Gibert recognized that fifteen-year-olds, because of their lack of worldly experience, did not have a body of materials for composition practice ready-to-hand. Their instructors had to provide it for them. So Gibert provided a fund of examples, strategies, and models for generating discourse. To see how invention was taught in the traditional classrooms of Gibert's day, one can examine the topics included and excluded in Gibert's treatment of invention.

In regard the oratorical arguments, Gibert was quite clear in his definition. Oratorical arguments used rational proofs to establish that which is doubtful. In an oratorical proof one posed a principle as true, applied it to a specific subject, and drew a conclusion from the application. The first type of proof discussed was the syllogism composed of three linked propositions of which the last was the conclusion. Its variants, the enthymeme (a rhetorical syllogism) and the epicheireme, were defined and exemplified. Gibert then distinguished between fallible and infallible signs and described three other argument types: dilemma, gradation, and conditional syllogism. Example, in which a particular fact was established from many similar facts relating to the same idea, was distinguished from induction, in which a general proposition was proved from enumeration of particulars. Gibert then discussed three methods of refutation: flat denial, simulated concession, and using an opponent's own premises against him (the "turnaround"). Further, guidelines for selecting arguments—suitability and adaptation to the audience and subject—were suggested.

Gibert's treatment of invention appeared to be a modified

form of the Aristotelian original. He moved slightly away from this model when it came to the *topoi* however. After listing them, he concluded, "these places are no good to a man who has no breeding, and when one is well bred, one does not need them anymore, in the same way that we need nothing to hold us up in water when we know how to swim."[5/b] With the exception of the topics, then, Gibert's discussion of invention retained all the standard neoclassical trappings: forms of deductive and inductive argument, taxonomies and distinctions between argumentative subforms, and specific strategies for refutation.

In the late seventeenth and early eighteenth centuries, treatments of invention like Gibert's disappeared in France. Most writers on rhetoric put aside treatment of argumentative proofs as something already known to readers (from the schools) and as a subject insufficiently interesting to merit attention. Hugh Blair's outlook was representative of a point of view widespread in both France and Britain: "though this study of the common places might produce very showy academical declamations, it could never produce useful discourses on real business. . . . What is truly solid and persuasive, must be drawn 'ex visceribus causae,' from a thorough knowledge of the subject, and profound meditation on it."[6] Unlike Gibert, Blair provided a brief treatment of the analytic and synthetic methods and then moved on to other matters, neglecting argumentative forms, refutation, and other concerns of *inventio*.

If Gibert represents the traditional, neoclassical approach to invention, Bernard Lamy provides the most striking example of a departure from it. Lamy produced a post-Cartesian account of argument that restricted it to formal proofs of syllogistic form. The speaker or writer seeking to adapt arguments to general audiences was advised to resort, not to argumentative proofs, but to narrative, portraiture, and clear and lively ideas. Lamy thus sought to supplement an attenuated inventional theory with elements that combined aesthetics and psychology in a mode of appeal that I shall call "the sixth

---

b. ces lieux ne servent de rien à un homme qui n'a point d'usage; & que quand on a quelque usage; on n'en a plus que faire: De la même maniere qu'on n'a plus besoin de rien qui nous soutienne dans l'eau, lorsque nous savons nager.

canon." Lamy's conception of the sixth canon illustrates a number of trends found in later belletristic rhetorics. Lamy was thus a significant transitional figure. The concepts and strategies suggested by him become commonplace in the eighteenth century. Even though Lamy's popularity in Britain was undermined by his Cartesianism, his indirect influence by way of later French rhetorics was considerable.

Bernard Lamy's *L'Art de parler*

Bernard Lamy, a seventeenth-century Oratorian, wrote numerous theoretical and pedagogical treatises on mathematics, science, and theology, but *L'Art de parler* is the work for which he is best known.[7] First published in 1676, the work appeared in over twenty French editions between 1675 and 1757 and in multiple editions in English translation during Lamy's lifetime and afterwards.[8] The work's signal influence for a century after its publication was shown by its extensive citation in the *Encyclopédie*'s article on "Rhétorique."[9]

Lamy was an acquaintance of the Port Royalists and Nicolas Malebranche, and his work was decidedly influenced by Descartes' philosophy and Port Royalist logic. Lamy's Cartesian sympathies caused him to be exiled briefly to Grenoble in 1675 because he failed to conform to the Oratorian policy of adherence to the Aristotelianism of Saint Thomas.[10] Although Lamy circumspectly avoided mention of Descartes' name in his rhetoric, Cartesian influence was pervasive throughout. For example, Lamy carefully followed Descartes' injunction to begin with the elements of one's subject that are the most simple and easiest to know and to progress by degrees to those which are more complex and difficult to understand.[11] Lamy took care to devote the first parts of his treatise to such fundamental matters as the physiology of the voice, the parts of speech, and the syntax of sentences. Only then did he proceed to more complex matters like elements of style and appeals to the passions. Furthermore, the passions Lamy treated were those considered most important by Descartes—admiration, esteem, and contempt. These and other Cartesian aspects of *L'Art de parler* have been described extensively by Le Guern and Thomas Carr.[12] However, those authors have only briefly treated Lamy's work in regard to the topic discussed here—the attenuation of invention in his rhetoric and its replacement with a psycho-physiological account of how discourse works immediately and involuntarily upon the mind.

L'Art de parler *as a Precursor of Belletrism*

L'Art de parler anticipated belletristic rhetorics in a number of senses. One of these was the breadth of its scope.[13] Lamy intended his art to include communication in all the humanistic disciplines. In his Preface, he noted that "this treatise is not intended for the Orator alone, but in general for all that either speak or write; for Poets, Historians, Philosophers, Divines, & c.[14/c] According to Lamy, the object of his work was *"les belles lettres"* or what was called by the Greeks *philologia,* and he believed that style was a general art applicable to all discursive forms. In his 1699 edition, Lamy took exception to critics who had suggested that he rename his work "L'Art de bien parler pour persuader," which would have implied that persuasion was a specific, delimited genre of discourse. Rather, Lamy felt that persuading was part and parcel of all efforts to communicate, since we always seek to influence and impress anyone to whom we speak: "One only employs the art to achieve one's ends: we speak only to cause those who hear us to share our sentiments; [to persuade] is the intention of all those who apply themselves to speaking well."[15/d]

A second sense in which Lamy's work anticipated later belletrism was his interest in studying forms of expression so as to find out more about how the mind works and about human nature in general. On this view, discourse itself had a sign relation to the mental operations that formed it; by studying the discourse, one could better understand the psycho-physiological processes of which it was an enactment. Lamy justified his treatise in part by saying, "I make several important reflections

---

c. Cet Ouvrage ne regarde pas seulement les Orateurs, mais generalement tous ceux qui parlent & qui écrivent, les Poëtes, les Historiens, les Philosophes, les Theologiens.

d. On n'emploïe l'Art que pour aller à ses fins: nous ne parlons que pour faire entrer dans nos sentimens ceux qui nous écoutent; [persuader] c'est l'intention qu'ont tous ceux qui s'appliquent à bien parler.

upon our mind, of which discourse is the image, which, contributing to our knowledge of ourselves, deserve our attention."[16/e]

Lamy also resembled the belletrists in his reductionist view of the mind's operations. While Lamy's psychology was based on that of René Descartes and while Scottish theories were allied with associationism, the implications of both for persuasion theory were nearly the same.[17] Both Cartesian and associationist psychology emphasized immediate, involuntary responses to discourse and discounted cognitive, rational responses. Both psychologies viewed the mind as a repository of past imprints that could be called up by sights and sounds that repeat or are associated with experiences in the present.

Descartes believed that the site of the excitation of the passions was the pineal gland located in the center of the brain. As the seat of the soul, this gland activated the animal spirits which served as a sort of transmission medium carrying sensory and other stimuli to the brain via the nerve paths. Descartes' psychology was mechanistic: the animal spirits resemble a hydraulic fluid; they leave imprints on the brain; they wear paths through frequency; they cause involuntary movements that can be viewed as outward signs of inward conditions. For example, admiration causes muscular fixation; love and hate cause thinning and thickening of the blood; and joy causes swelling of the lungs.[18]

The language and the cast of Lamy's description of persuasion clearly reflected Cartesian psychology. Lamy argued that discourse should be designed to mirror experience, to call up the passions a rhetor wishes to evoke by setting forth the sounds and images with which those passions are associated: "Every motion that is made in the Organs of the Sense, and communicated to the Animal Spirits, is connext by the God of Nature, to some certain motion of the Soul; Sound can excite passions, and we may say, that every passion answers to some sound or other; which is it, that excites in the Animal Spirits, the motion wherewith it is allyed."[19/f]

---

e. je fais plusieurs reflexions importantes sur nostre esprit, dont le discours est l'image, qui pouvant contribuër à nous faire entrer dans la connoissance de ce que nous sommes, meritent que l'on y fasse attention.

f. Chaque mouvement qui se fait dans les organes des sens, & qui est communiqué aux esprits animaux ayant este lié par l'Auteur de la nature à un

Since rhetorical response was thus nearly automatic, nearly involuntary, Lamy's aim was to discover the discursive triggers that excited the desired emotional responses. As Jean-Paul Sermain observed, "When B. Lamy describes the manner in which the movements of the will are inscribed in discourse, it is because he considers possible the inverse path: in arranging words in such a fashion as to represent the marks of sensibility, one can act on the affectivity of others. For the caprice of circumstances or genius, rhetoric substitutes sure laws that permit the orator to foresee the reactions of the auditor and thus 'program' his behavior."[20/g]

One of Lamy's aims, then, was to articulate the means by which expression and sounds could incite certain reactions in the audience. For Lamy, the marks of passion in discourse took the forms of tropes and figures. Ellipsis, for example, showed a passion so violent that it could not be articulated; exclamation revealed excitement and impetuosity; and apostrophe indicated a compelling need for succor. Elements of delivery could likewise excite like-minded states in hearers. Equality and order in cadence could produce a calming effect, whereas bad pronunciation and discordant sounds could cause discomfort. Because he believed that stylistic figures and the articulation of sounds caused direct and involuntary effects on hearers, Lamy devoted the second and third parts of his treatise (respectively) to these two topics. These two parts alone accounted for nearly one half of *L'Art de parler*'s first edition.

Invention in L'Art de parler

In a system such as Lamy's where an audience's passions could be aroused directly by sensible impressions and vivid description, very little room was left for invention in the tradi-

---

certain mouvement de l'ame, les sons peuvent exciter les passions, & l'on peut dire que chacune répond à un certain son qui est celuy qui excite dans les esprits animaux le mouvement avec lequel elle est liée.

g. Quand B. Lamy décrit la manière dont les mouvements de la volonté s'inscrivent dans le discours, c'est parce qu'il estime possible le chemin inverse: en agençant les mots de façon à y faire figurer les marques de la sensibilité, on peut agir sur l'affectivité des autres. Au caprice des circonstances ou du génie, la rhétorique substitue des lois sûres qui permettent à l'orateur de prévoir les réactions de l'auditeur et donc de 'programmer' son comportement.

tional sense. Lamy's view of invention was influenced not only by Descartes' psycho-physiological account of how the mind worked but also by a Cartesian conception of truth. Lamy's assumption was that truth was or should be ascertained prior to the rhetorical act; the rhetor's job was to make it known to his hearers. This was typical of belletristic rhetorics where invention worked to make known truths apparent rather than to establish truths through proofs. Lamy thus viewed the substance of discourse as managerial rather than epistemic.[21] "To persuade," Lamy observed, "we must find a way to bring People to our Sentiments that were of a contrary sentiment before: We must put our matter in Order in our minds, and having fairly disposed it, we must make choice of such words as are proper to express it."[22/h]

The Cartesian nature of this truth was further apparent in its unicity. Like Descartes, Lamy believed that only one view was true and only one truth was right.[23] The issue was not to arrive at a considered decision based on probabilities and social, legal, or moral principle. Instead, the persuader was to make a known truth visible to his audience: "If men loved the truth . . . and if they searched for it sincerely, one would need only to propose it simply and artlessly to have them accept it, but they hate it and, because it does not accommodate their interests, they voluntarily blind themselves so as not to see it."[24/i]

Such willfully obtuse resistance could be overcome only through an orator's concentrated effort to make truth both clear and attractive to his audience. Lamy recommended proof through demonstration combined with more surreptitious and crafty methods. The forms of proof put forward as exemplary in Lamy's discussion of invention were syllogistic and deductive as he followed the Port Royalists' emphasis upon categorical

---

h. Pour persuader, il faut trouver les moyens de faire tomber dans son sentiment ceux qui sont dans un sentiment contraire. On doit mettre en ordre ce que l'on a trouvé; & aprés avoir disposé en son esprit toutes choses, il faut employer les paroles propres pour communiquer les pensées que l'on a euës.

i. Si les hommes aimoient la verité . . . & s'ils la cherchoient sincerement il ne feroit besoin pour la leur faire recevoir que de la leur proposer simplement & sans art, mais ils la haïssent, & parce qu'elle ne s'accommode pas avec leurs interests, ils s'aveuglent volontairement pour ne la pas voir.

and other syllogistic forms.[25] Part 1 of *L'Art de parler* described reasoning or argumentation in this way: "We argue, when from one or two clear and evident Propositions, we conclude the truth or falsity of a third Proposition that is obscure and disputable. As if to prove the innocence of Milo we should say thus: It is lawful to repel force by force, Milo, in killing Clodius, did only repel force by force; Ergo, Milo did lawfully kill Clodius."[26/j] Cicero's categorical syllogism, taken from *Pro Milone,* was here and elsewhere used in *L'Art de parler* as exemplary of the sort of reasoning Lamy recommended.[27] It was deployed again in Lamy's explicit discussion of invention where he concluded that the principal form of reasoning was to "make use of one or more incontestable Propositions, and make it appear that the Proposition contested is the same with those which are incontestable. . . ."[28/k] The major benefit of such a tightly constructed, conservative argument was, of course, its indubitability. "In an exact Argument the Principles and Consequences are joyn'd so strictly, that having granted the Principles, we are oblig'd to consent to the Consequence, because the Principles and the Consequence are the same thing; so that we cannot reasonably deny in the one what we have confess'd in the other."[29/l]

In Lamy's inventional system, then, arguments from strict deduction were the preferred form of rhetorical reasoning and the only real means of establishing a speaker's thesis. Arguments using the commonplaces and the topics did not function as forms of proof but only as means of amplifying or filling out the speaker's treatment of a subject. Commonplaces were conceived by Lamy as standard propositions or themes to be am-

---

j. Nous raisonnons lorsque d'une ou de deux propositions claires & evidentes, nous concluons la verité ou la fausseté d'une troisiéme proposition obscure & contestée. Comme si pour prouver que Milon est innocent, nous disons: Il est permis de repousser la force par la force; Milon en tuant Clodius, n'a fait que repousser la force par la force; donc Milon a pû tuer Clodius.

k. se servir d'une ou de plusieurs propositions qui ne souffrent aucune difficulté & leur faire voir que cette proposition contestée est la meme que celles qui sont incontestables.

l. Dans un raisonnement exact les principes & les consequences, sont si étroitement liez qu'on est obligé d'accorder la consequence, ayant consenti aux principes, puisque les principes, & la consequence ne sont qu'une meme chose, ainsi l'on ne peut pas nier raisonnablement ce que l'on a une fois accordé.

plified and decorated. In this function, he observed, they had
their uses: "They make us take notice of several things from
whence Arguments may be drawn; they teach us how a subject
may be vary'd and discovered on all sides. If . . . an Orator be
ignorant, and understands not the bottom of what he treats, he
can speak but superficially, he cannot come to the point, and
after he has talk'd and argued a long time [by making use of
commonplaces], his Adversary will have reason to admonish
him to leave his tedious talk that signifies nothing. . . ."[30/m]
Thus did Lamy set aside the probative function of commonplaces and claim that they merely furnished the means of amplification to speakers largely ignorant of their subject.

Lamy's disparagement of the topics was, of course, a departure from the classical tradition. Aristotle's *Topica* functioned
as a compendium of procedures and lines of argument by which
to argue constructively or destructively about recurring issues
in dialectical debates.[31] Cicero's *Topica* was meant to be a similar treatise.[32] French treatises of the early modern period
nonetheless said very little that was favorable to the theory of
commonplaces. Lamy condemned them and so did Arnauld and
Nicole.[33] Lamy reminded his readers that there was no easy
way to knowledge, that what was required was "serious meditation, and long study, of which few men were capable."[34/n]
The commonplaces served those who "sought out short and
easy ways to supply themselves with matter of discourse. . . ."[35/o] Fénelon, too, had noted that the person who has
limited preparation is "reduced to paying off in the currency of
aphorisms and antitheses, treat[s] only the commonplaces, utter[s] nothing but incoherencies and . . . do[es] not show the
real principles of things."[36/p]

------

m. ils font prendre garde à plusieurs choses dont on peut tirer des argu-
mens; ils montrent comme l'on peut tourner un sujet de tous côtez, & l'envisa-
ger par toutes ses faces. Si un Orateur ignore le fond de la matiere qu'il traite,
il ne peut atteindre que la surface des choses, il ne touchera point le noeud de
l'affaire; de sorte qu'aprés avoir parlé long temps, son adversaire aura sujet de
lui dire. . . . Finissez ces grands discours qui ne disent rien. . . .

n. serieuses meditations, & par de longues études dont peu de gens sont
capables.

o. ont cherché des moyens courts & faciles pour trouver de la matiere de
discourir. . . .

p. réduit à payer de phrases et d'antithèses; on ne traite que des lieux

Like his Port Royalist predecessors, Lamy nevertheless listed fifteen of the commonplaces but provided a discussion of them so brief as to hardly be worth the effort.[37] He also listed general topics for deliberative, judicial, and demonstrative speaking. Nevertheless, he indicated his fundamental rejection of the topical method of invention by arguing that the skilled orator, when faced with a hostile or skeptical audience, would be best advised to be selective, committing himself to a single, telling argument rather than diffusing his efforts through a system of topically based arguments that would have the effect of "ill weeds that choke the corn."[q] He concluded that "we need but one Argument, if it be solid and strong, and that Eloquence consists in clearing of that, and making it perspicuous."[38/r]

Lamy's writings on invention revealed a conception of and dependence on argument that was formal, deductive, demonstrative, and indisputable. In this his views were Cartesian. The only arguments viewed as cogent were the ones that depended on proofs like those of formal logic or mathematics. By contrast, classical invention had focused on the functionings of public argument using audience beliefs and probabilities—bases which would provide enthymematic and exemplary structures as the logical underpinnings of discourse. Classical writers did not suppose there were irrefutable "truths" on which public argument could be based, but for Lamy, the truth was decided upon prior to speaking; the orator's task was to make the truth clear; and his means was to argue syllogistically from an incontestable proposition to an indubitable conclusion. Even then, however, auditors might hate the truth if it was incompatible with their personal interests.

The Psychological Dimensions of Persuasion

Lamy's adoption of Cartesian rationalism and his disparagement of probabilistic inductive reasoning meant that he must recommend some other recourse for orators faced with

---

communs, on ne dit rien que de vague, et . . . ne montre point les vrais principes des choses.

    q. de mauvaises herbes qui étouffent la bonne semence.

    r. Il n'est besoin que d'une seule preuve qui soit forte & solide, & que l'éloquence consiste à étendre cette preuve, & la mettre en son jour, afin qu'elle soit apperçûë.

recalcitrant, inattentive audiences. Somehow speakers must transform such groups into people who were attentive and amenable to persuasion. This was where the orator's task differed from the philosopher's. The philosopher need only convince and make the truth apparent, whereas the orator must use *l'adresse* ("craft" or "cunning") and vivacity of expression to genuinely persuade.

In Lamy's system, *l'adresse* was a psychological device of using people's inclinations to change their inclinations. To succeed in this strategy, the speaker would identify those audience values relevant to his cause and manipulate them into premises favoring his thesis, thereby changing the audience's view without their being aware of it. Or, as Lamy described it, "when one proposes things contrary to the inclinations of those to whom one speaks, craft is necessary. One can only worm one's way into their minds by diverse and secret paths. That is why one must act so that they perceive the truth only after it is the mistress of their hearts; otherwise they will close the door of their minds as to an enemy. . . ."[39/s]

Lamy believed that this process of insinuation was not necessarily dishonest. Rather, one could proceed by locating those elements in a given view coincident with one's own and make use of them in subtle and disingenuous ways. "There is no Opinion whatever in which all things are either false or unreasonable: Without offence to the truth, we may side at first with that Opinion which we design to subvert, by commending in it that which is true, and worthy of commendations."[40/t] Lamy did not hesitate to provide concrete examples of such a strategy. One might dissuade a vain woman from using makeup by saying that it is harmful to her skin.[41] Or one might note the ex-

---

s. . . . lorsque l'on propose des choses contraires aux inclinations de ceux à qui on parle, l'adresse est necessaire. L'on ne peut s'insinuer dans leur esprit que par des chemins écartez & secrets; c'est pourquoi il faut faire ensorte qu'ils n'apperçoivent point la verité dont on veut les persuader qu'aprés qu'elle sera maîtresse de leur coeur; autrement ils lui fermeront la porte de leur esprit, comme à une ennemie. . . .

t. Dans une opinion quelle qu'elle soit, tout n'est pas faux, tout n'est pas déraisonnable: on peut sans blesser la verité s'attacher d'abord à ce qui en est vray dans l'opinion que l'on veut combattre, & la loüer en ce qu'elle a de veritable, & qui merite des loüanges."

ample of Christ who reassured the traditional Jewry that he was not there to overturn the law but to fulfill it.[42]

The need to understand human nature and human psychology meant that, in Lamy's view, rhetoric and the art of persuasion were inappropriate objects of study for schoolboys and for teaching by rote. "'Tis true the art of working upon an Auditory is much above the reach of a young Schollar, for whom the antient Rhetoricks were properly made. This Art is acquir'd by sublime speculations, by reflexions upon the nature of our mind, upon our inclinations, and motions of our will. 'Tis the fruit of Experience and long Observation of the manner wherewith men act and govern themselves. . . ."[43/u] Here we see a nascent psychology as well as an effort to construct an account of persuasion consistently connected to Lamy's understanding of how the mind worked and how it responded to discursive stimuli.

As I have noted, Lamy's Cartesian conception of the mind's operations caused him to view audience responses to discourse as immediate and involuntary. The function of style was not simply to lend coloring or to make speech attractive. Style was what gave discourse a sensory quality and thereby the capacity to make impressions on the mind. "The tropes," said Lamy, "are a sensible painting of the thing of which one speaks."[44/v] Furthermore, appeals to the senses, for which the figures and tropes are the only means, are vital. "Ordinarily we do not like abstract truths that are perceived only by the eyes of the mind. We are so accustomed to conceive only by means of our senses that we are incapable of using our minds alone and of understanding reasoning if it is not established upon some sensible experience: that is why abstract expressions are enigmas to most people; and that those please them which are sensible and which form in the imagination a painting of the thing that is to be conceived."[45/w] To make an impression on the mind,

---

u. Il est vrai que la science de gagner les coeurs est bien au dessus de la portée d'un jeune écolier, pour lequel on fait des Rhetoriques: Elle s'acquiert par de sublimes speculations, par des reflexions sur la nature de nôtre esprit, sur les inclinations, sur les mouvemens de nôtre volunté. C'est le fruit d'une longue experience qu'on a fait de la maniere que les hommes agissent & qu'ils se gouvernent. . . .

v. Les tropes sont une peinture sensible de la chose dont on parle.

w. On n'aime pas ordinairement les veritez abstraites qui ne s'apperçoi-

then, a speaker's thoughts must be converted into a form that can be sensed or felt. Synecdoches convert the abstract into the concrete; metaphors enliven conception through striking associations; and hyperboles enlarge our ideas of things by associating them with grand objects. Figures and tropes agitate the soul, excite the animal spirits, and stimulate the passions so that the audience is swayed to the affective state desired by the orator. This process was described by Lamy as he considered the persuasive effects of style:

> When the outward Object strikes upon our Sense, the motion it makes is communicated by the Nerves to the very Centre of the Brain, whose substance being soft, receives thereby certain prints and impressions: The alliance or Connexion betwixt the Mind and the Body, is the cause that the Ideas of Corporal things are annex'd to these prints. . . . We may call those Prints the Images of the Objects. The power the Soul has to form upon the Brain the Images of things that have been perceiv'd, is called Imagination, which word signifies both that power of the Soul, and the Images that it forms.[46/x]

Vivacity is attained through imagery. Imagery creates pictures that re-present reality and make direct impressions upon the brain. These impressions become associated with ideas and thereby convey a general thought that the hearer can later recall. Lamy's account anticipated later versions of association-

---

vent que par les yeux de l'esprit. Nous sommes tellement accoûtumez à ne concevoir que par les sens, que nous sommes incapables de faire usage de nostre pur esprit, & comprendre un raisonnement, s'il n'est établi sur quelque experience sensible: de là vient que les expressions abstraites sont des Enigmes à la plupart des gens; & que celles-là plaisent qui sont sensibles, & qui forment dans l'imagination une peinture de la chose qu'on leur veut faire concevoir.

x. Lorsque les objets exterieurs frappent nos sens, le mouvement que ces objets y excitent, se communiquent par le moyen des nerfs jusques au centre du cerveau, dont la substance molle reçoit par cette impression de certaines traces. L'étroite liaison qui est entre l'ame & le corps, fait que les idées des choses corporelles sont liées avec ces traces. . . . Nous pouvons appeler ces traces les images des objets. La puissance qu'a l'ame de former sur le cerveau les images des choses qu'on a une fois apperceuës, s'appelle l'imagination: & ce mot signifie en même temps, & cette puissance de l'ame & ces images qu'elle forme.

ism. Like the belletrists of the eighteenth century, Lamy believed that an idea had to be made palpable and concrete to be understood and remembered and that stylistic dimensions of discourse enabled associations by calling up desired images from the soul's repository.

Vraisemblance

Manifest in Lamy's work was a preoccupation with *vraisemblance* or verisimilitude and *bienséance* or propriety. As I shall show in chapter 2, these two critical *topoi* became common in the rhetorics of Smith, Blair, and Campbell. They constituted persuasion's intellective dimension for these theorists and received much more press than its argumentative dimension. *Bienséance* had its origin in social practices and mores. Were forms of address suited to the stature of the persons involved? Did the characters portrayed in a narrative appropriately observe social conventions? Were forms of their expression suited to the subject matter and occasion? *Vraisemblance* was related to whether the account was, literally speaking, "seemingly true," or whether it conformed to its audiences' expectations. Did the events portrayed seem probable given listeners' past experience? Were they sequenced in a manner that seemed natural? Were the customs and mores matched to the time period in question?

An account was said to possess verisimilitude if its premises were held to be true by the audience. Unlike the geometer, the orator could look to the audience's cultural beliefs in constructing arguments. Statements such as "everyone should get his due" and "it is impossible for a thing to be and not to be at the same time" had verisimilitude because they would go unquestioned. The orator could fit them together and expect them mutually to fortify one another.

Propriety also contributed to discursive effectiveness. In regard to arrangement, authors must strive for proportion and appropriateness so that the parts of a discourse were mutually suited. "Every thing is to be allowed its natural dimension. A Statue whose parts are disproportionate, whose leggs are great, and arms small, whose body is large and head small, is monstrous and irregular."[47/y] Likewise, figures and tropes

---

y. Il faut donner à chaque chose son étendue naturelle: une statue dont

should be suited to the thought conveyed. While not literal, figures and tropes contributed to discursive effect by interpreting and coloring the meanings of "true" details. For example, a speaker wishing to give an idea of a very high rock would not fully accomplish this aim by using such terms as "large" or "lofty." Such expression is not extraordinary, however true literally. One might better say "It threatened the heavens." The hyperbole would be appropriate because it expressed the exceptional grandeur of the idea.[48] Expression thus should be attuned to the passion conveyed. "There is nothing comes nearer Folly than to be transported without Cause; to put one self into a heat for a thing that ought to be argued coolly; each Motion has its Figures."[49/z] Every choice a speaker makes about the form of expression should be governed by the nature of the matter in question so that style is consistently functional. Simple matters should be simply expressed, while more complicated and abstract principles should be made concrete and carefully related to each other.

Vraisemblance lent both an intellective and an aesthetic dimension to discursive influence. Intellectually, the audience member would tacitly consider the commensurability with existing experience and expectations of the speech's style, its narrative, and its arrangement. Aesthetically, the recipient could appreciate the artfulness of a construction as instantiated in its appropriateness. "If one reflects a little about this," Lamy observed, "one will find that the pleasure one has in a well-made discourse is caused only by this resemblance which one finds between the image that the words form in the mind and the things of which they are the painting, so that it is either the truth that pleases or the conformity of words with things."[50/aa]

---

les parties ne sont pas proportionnées, qui a de grandes jambes & de petits bras, un petit corps & une grosse teste, est monstrueuse. . . .

z. Il n'y a rien qui approche plus de la folie que de se laisser aller à des emportemens sans aucun sujet, de se mettre en colere pour une chose qu'on doit traitter avec froideur; chaque mouvement a ses figures.

aa. Si on refléchit un peu sur ce sentiment, on trouvera que le plaisir que l'on prend dans un discours bien-fait n'est causé que par cette ressemblance, qui se trouve entre l'image que les paroles forment dans l'esprit & les choses dont elles sont la peinture; de sorte que c'est la verité qui plaist, ou la conformité des paroles avec les choses.

L'Art de parler *as a Transitional Rhetoric*

It has been said of René Descartes that everything that pre-ceded him was "old"; everything that came after was "new."[51] The same could be said of Lamy's rhetoric. Based as it was upon Cartesian psychology and upon a Cartesian conception of truth, Lamy's work constituted a radical departure from the scholastic and neoclassical rhetorics that preceded it. Further, Lamy's was an adult rhetoric, written for literate readers who sought to express themselves well and clearly. It consequently disparaged the commonplaces merely as a means of amplifica-tion and sought to supplant them with a deductive method of proof more like geometry than probabilistic reasoning. It also recognized eloquence as a sophisticated practice that could suc-ceed only if its practitioner knew the basic principles of psy-chology and the strategies of *l'adresse*.

L'Art de parler functioned as a precursor to later belletris-tic rhetorics along many dimensions. Its scope was broad, treat-ing discourse in all the *belles lettres*—history, philosophy, and poetics as well as rhetoric. It considered the workings of dis-course as a means of understanding the workings of the mind that produced it. Since it viewed hearers' responses to dis-course as immediate and often involuntary rather than cogni-tive, *L'Art de parler* emphasized aesthetic dimensions of eloquence such as vivacity, clarity, and portraiture because of their capacity to appeal to the senses. In all this, Lamy's work anticipated the later rhetorics of the Scottish Enlightenment.

One must note, however, that Smith, Campbell and Blair did not cite Lamy.[52] Rather, they turned for their inspiration to his contemporaries and immediate successors—Fénelon, Bou-hours, Boileau, and Dubos. The remainder of this chapter will explain how these later theorists developed and extended the themes that initially appeared in Lamy's rhetoric. The role of Lamy's work can best be characterized as representative of in-tellectual currents arising in late seventeenth- and early eigh-teenth-century France and as anticipatory of many later trends in the belletristic rhetorics of the eighteenth century.

The Sixth Canon: A New Theory of Influence

Belletristic rhetorics, including Lamy's, focused on recep-tion, not production. Their aim was to develop the "man of taste" among their readers. To do so, they described the features of discourse that caused pleasure and made an impression. They were specially concerned with such aesthetic features as clarity, vivacity, verisimilitude, and propriety. These aesthetic elements preoccupied Lamy's peers and immediate successors as they took up his interest in the psychological dimensions of persuasion and the cognitive processes involved.

Fénelon, Bouhours, Rollin, and Dubos considered poetry and oratory to be like portraiture. In their view, discourse ought to re-present experience, and the re-presentation should be proportionate to the original. If there were consistent correlations between reality and conceptions of it, thought and the modes of its expression, and recipients' experience and the narratives they heard, then discourse would have aesthetic appeal because of the proportionality of its representations. And only by causing pleasure could discourse have effect. When presented with an artful (i.e., vivid, appropriate, and verisimilar) re-presentation, the man of taste would intuitively and immediately respond to its aesthetic qualities and be influenced by them. The capacity for such reception, called by Dubos a "sixth sense," will be further discussed in chapter 4. Dubos attributed this capacity to any educated person and said of it that "it is, in short, what is commonly called sentiment. The heart acts on its own and by a movement that precedes all deliberation when the object presented to it really is touching, whether it be real or an imitation. The heart is made, is organized, for that. Its operation thus forestalls all reasoning. . . ."[53/bb] This sixth sense, later adopted by Francis Hutcheson and his successors, had the effect of replacing cognition and deliberative judgment.[54]

Oratory as Portraiture

To be moved by discourse, one's senses and imagination must be stimulated. Sensory appeals that are stimulating af-

---

bb. Le coeur s'agite de lui même & par un mouvement qui précéde toute délibération, quand l'objet qu'on lui presente est rééllement un objet touchant, soit que l'objet ait une existence réelle, soit qu'il soit un objet imité. Le coeur est fait, il est organisé pour cela. Son opération prévient donc tous les raisonnements. . . .

fect the passions and cause auditors to experience orators' images and thus their ideas. Like Lamy, Fénelon, Bouhours, Rollin, and Dubos all emphasized vivid depiction and visualization. Rollin insisted, for example, that one of the greatest beauties in discourse consisted of giving "substance and reality to the things of which one speaks, and in painting them with visible strokes that strike the senses, move the imagination, and reveal a sensible object."[55/cc]

Among the theorists applying visualist metaphors to oratory, none was more eloquent than Fénelon who blurred the demarcation between poetry and oratory by applying to the latter aesthetic criteria usually reserved for painting and portraiture. Fénelon believed that the "true speaker," the one who knows how to enter the hearts of others and win them over, knows how to paint with words:

> To portray is not only to describe things but to represent their surrounding features in so lively and so concrete a way that the listener imagines himself almost seeing them. . . . When [Virgil] assembles all the surrounding features of [Dido's] despair, when he shows you the savage Dido, the lineaments of death already etched upon her face, when he makes her speak with her eyes upon Aeneas' portrait and upon his sword, your imagination transports you to Carthage, you believe that you see the Trojan fleet receding from the beach and the queen whom nothing can console. . . . the poet disappears. You see nothing but that which he makes visible . . . There one sees the power of imitation and of portraiture!"[56/dd]

---

cc. du corps et de la réalité aux choses dont on parle, et à les peindre par des traits visibles qui frappent les sens, qui remuent l'imagination, et qui montrent un objet sensible.

dd. Peindre, c'est non-seulement décrire les choses, mais en représenter les circonstances d'une manière si vive et si sensible, que l'auditeur s'imagine presque les voir. . . . Quand [Virgile] ramasse toutes les circonstances de ce désespoir [de Didon], qu'il vous montre Didon furieuse, avec un visage où la mort est déjà peinte, qu'il la fait parler à la vue de ce portrait et de cette épée, votre imagination vous transporte à Carthage; vous croyez voir la flotte des Troyens qui fuit le rivage, et la reine que rien n'est capable de consoler. . . . Le poëte disparoît; on ne voit plus que ce qu'il fait voir. . . . Voilà la force de l'imitation et de la peinture.

Fénelon then argued that portraiture must be a part of eloquence as of poetry, for "a simple story cannot move. It is necessary, not only to acquaint the listeners with the facts, but to make the facts visible to them, and to strike their consciousness by means of a perfect representation of the arresting manner in which the facts have come to pass."[57/ee] As Wilbur Samuel Howell has remarked, for Fénelon, oratory was almost but not quite poetry, since no discourse could have a persuasive effect without portraiture.[58]

Dubos' description of the persuasive effects of portraiture was perhaps the most detailed. In the first volume of his *Réflexions critiques,* Dubos explained that what gives pleasure is the knowledge that the object being portrayed is not the real object but an imitation. Instead of real experience, what impresses us is the artfulness of the imitation. "It is in virtue of the power that imitation draws from nature that the real object acts upon us. . . . The pleasure that one feels in seeing imitations . . . is a pure pleasure. It is not followed by the troubles that would have been caused by serious emotions accompanying the real object."[59/ff] The aesthetic distance afforded by our knowledge that what we experience is an imitation is itself enjoyable. Furthermore, the artificial passions inspired by an imitation resemble real passions and thus leave an impression: "Painters and poets excite in us these artificial passions, by presenting to us imitations of objects that are capable of exciting real passions in us, for the impression that these imitations make on us is of the same kind as the [real] object. . . . But since the impression that the imitation makes is different from the impression that the [real] object would make only in that it is less strong, it must excite in our soul a passion which resembles the one that the [real] object could have excited."[60/gg]

---

ee. Un récit simple ne peut émouvoir: il faut non-seulement instruire les auditeurs des faits, mais les leur rendre sensibles, et frapper leurs sens par une représentation parfaite de la manière touchante dont ils sont arrivés.

ff. C'est en vertu du pouvoir qu'il tient de la nature même que l'objet réel agit sur nous. . . . Le plaisir qu'on sent à voir les imitations . . . est un plaisir pur. Il n'est pas suivi des inconvéniens dont les émotions serieuses qui auroient été causées par l'objet même seroient accompagnées.

gg. Les Peintres & les Poëtes excitent en nous ces passions artificielles, en nous présentant les imitations des objets qui sont capables d'exciter en nous

In Dubos' account, then, the power of portraiture arose from two sources—an audience's appreciation of the artfulness of imitation and the imitation's capacity to simulate actual experience, thus exciting the imagination and leaving an impression on the hearer. This emphasis upon visualist stimulation was compatible both with Cartesian psychology and with the introspective empiricism of the eighteenth century. Imitation and portraiture, thematized by the French belletrists, appeared again in the works of Smith, Campbell, Blair and others who emphasized the concrete, the specific, and the sensible.

Propriety

In Lamy's rhetoric, propriety was thematized by an insistence that style and expression be suited to the nature of the subject and of the passion expressed. As I will argue in chapter 2, propriety provided a central element in Fénelon's rhetorics which valorized unity, coherence, simplicity, and unobtrusiveness in self-expression. Nothing disturbed Fénelon more than the ostentatious floridity and artificial arrangement of epideictic speaking in his day.[61] Only by observing propriety and appropriateness in selecting materials, organizing sermons, avoiding unnecessary diversions, and crafting a suitable style could the preacher expect to avoid the excesses so common in seventeenth century speaking.

Fénelon was not alone in his concern for propriety; all the French belletrists were concerned with the seemly and the fitting. Dubos, for example, disparaged violation of what the Italians called *il costume,* the artist's or playwright's ability to depict characters in a manner conforming to their situations. Dubos defined *il costume* as following "what we know about the mores, clothes, buildings, and armaments particular to the peoples represented.[62/hh] Just as painters were to depict the scenes of a particular place or time in conformity with what

---

des passions véritables, car l'impression que ces imitations font sur nous est du même genre que l'impression [de] l'objet même. . . . Mais comme l'impression que l'imitation fait n'est differente de l'impression que l'objet imité feroit qu'en ce qu'elle est moins forte, elle doit exciter dans notre ame une passion qui ressemble à celle que l'objet imité y auroit pû exciter.

hh. ce que nous sçavons des moeurs, des habits, des bâtimens, & des armes particulieres des peuples qu'on veut réprésenter.

was known to have existed in those circumstances, so must orators and poets recount narratives and characters in a manner faithful to historical fact and social convention.

In any portrayal, the orator or artist should select those traits or features of the subject that show it in its true light. To be true to *bienséance,* the subject's elements should be configured and displayed so as to reveal its essential nature. Dubos illustrated this principle when he discussed how playwrights should form realistic and believable characters: "It is necessary to be capable of discerning among the twenty or thirty things that a man says or does the three or four traits that are especially proper to his particular character. One must gather these traits; and continuing to study his model, to extract from his actions and discourse those traits most proper to make his portrait known."[63/ii] The traits and actions selected and attributed by playwrights would be believable if they were suited to the character's circumstances, experience, and situation. To portray a shepherd or rustic person speaking in the sublime style, or to attribute effeminate or florid speech to a Roman soldier would violate this sense of *bienséance.*

Furthermore, the mode of expression should suit the subject at hand as well as the speaker's own character. Plain and simple matters called for a conversational style, whereas the grand style was to be reserved for significant or profound subjects or instances wherein an orator sought to invoke strong passions. The positions of various theorists on the role of the figures of speech in the grand style were somewhat mixed. Lamy had believed that figured speech was the language of the passions, and he had considered the tropes and figures as resources for appealing to the imagination. Bouhours, however, argued that he listened to sermons to be instructed, not to be entertained by *bagatelles* so inappropriate to religious eloquence.[64] While Fénelon followed Cicero and St. Augustine in discussing the simple, moderate, and grand styles of speaking, he sought almost immediately to separate floridity from sub-

---

ii. il faut être capable de discerner entre vingt ou trente choses que dit, ou que fait un homme, trois ou quatre traits qui sont propres spécialement à son caractere particulier. Il faut ramasser ces traits; & continuant d'étudier son modele, extraire, pour ainsi dire, de ses actions & de ses discours les traits les plus propres à faire reconnoître le portrait.

lime expression.[65] "I confess that the florid style has its charms, but they are misplaced in discourses which do not call for refined witticisms and in which great passions must be expressed. The florid style never attains the sublime."[66/jj] Elsewhere, Fénelon extended this idea by noting that an instinctive sensitivity to propriety of style was a surer sign of eloquence than floridity. "Most men who wish to make beautiful utterances seek indiscriminately throughout to have pomposity of language. . . . They aspire only to strew their speech with ornaments, like bad cooks who know nothing about how to put in proper seasoning. . . . True eloquence has nothing of the inflated or ambitious. She moderates and proportions herself to the subjects which she treats and to the men whom she instructs. She is only mighty and sublime when she must be."[67/kk]

Vraisemblance

As noted before, that which has the quality of *vraisemblance* appears to be true to listeners or readers because it conforms to their past experience and to their expectations of what is normal and natural. Insofar as the seemingly true relates to social custom, dress, and proprieties of social behavior, *bienséance* is related to *vraisemblance*. But *vraisemblance* is a broader and more inclusive concept and arises from the congruence of facts and events in a text, the completeness with which circumstances are reported, and the general familiarity or believability of portrayals. In its preoccupation with the manner of expression and the artfulness of portrayal, *bienséance* is an aesthetic criterion, whereas verisimilitude deals with the "logic" of a work.

---

jj. J'avoue que le genre fleuri a ses grâces; mais elles sont déplacées dans les discours où il ne s'agit point d'un jeu d'esprit plein de délicatesse et où les grandes passions doivent parler. Le genre fleuri n'atteint jamais au sublime.

kk. La plupart des gens qui veulent faire de beaux discours cherchent sans choix également partout la pompe des paroles. . . . [I]ls ne songent qu'à charger leurs discours d'ornements; semblables aux méchants cuisiniers, qui ne savent rien assaisonner avec justesse. . . . La véritable éloquence n'a rien d'enflé ni d'ambitieux; elle se modère, et se proportionne aux sujets qu'elle traite et aux gens qu'elle instruit; elle n'est grande et sublime que quand il faut l'être.

The concerns of French belletrism remind us that nearly all discourse has narrative elements. Speeches in a sense tell a story and invite their audiences to piece events together in the way desired by the orator and to draw conclusions based on this account. Histories are reported through the lens of the historian-as-storyteller who selects and relates events so as to display a particular perspective of what happened. To the extent that discourse operates narratively, verisimilitude as a criterion is applicable to it. Audiences expect narratives to unfold in certain sequences; they expect specific persons to act in conformity with their characters; and they expect all circumstances pertinent to an action to be reported. Descriptions and accounts lacking these qualities lack *vraisemblance*.

The French conception of *vraisemblance* emerged from a conception of what was "natural"—what conformed to past experience and present expectation. Rollin reminded his readers of the importance of this capacity in judging descriptions: "the surest means of succeeding . . . is to consult nature, to study it well, to take it for a guide in such a way that each feels in himself the truth of what is said and finds in his own depths the sentiments expressed in the discourse."[68/ll] Bouhours agreed that there was a certain capacity in listeners and readers that caused them to respond favorably to what was true in what they heard and read: "When we read something true, it is neither the book nor the author that causes us to find it true; it is something we carry in ourselves well raised above substances and perceptible intelligence, and which is an impression, a springing forth of the eternal light of truth."[69/mm]

Narratively, *vraisemblance* evolved from the way circumstances were ordered and sequenced. In configuring a narrative's elements, a writer must prepare the way for later developments by introducing early events judiciously. In order

---

ll. le moyen le plus sûr de réussir . . . est de consulter la nature, de la bien étudier, de la prendre pour guide, en sorte que chacun sente en soi même la vérité de ce qu'on dit, et trouve dans son propre fonds les sentimens qui sont exprimés dans le discours.

mm. Quand nous lisons quelque chose de vray, ce n'est ni le livre, ni l'Auteur qui nous le fait trouver vray; c'est quelque chose que nous portons en nousmesmes de bien élevé au dessus des corps & de la lumière sensible, & qui est une impression, un rejaillissement de la lumière éternelle de la vérité.

to interpret and understand the crux of an account, its recipients must know what preceded it. Fénelon emphasized this quality in his discussion of the historian's art. He observed that "the truly talented historian . . . chooses from twenty possible spots the one where a fact will be best placed to shed light on all the others. Often an event set forth long before it happened will clear up everything that prepares the way for it. Often another event will be better put to light when held until the end. By being presented later, it emerges more opportunely as the cause of other events."[70/nn]

The significance of an audience's prior experience and understanding in *vraisemblance* was also illustrated by the correspondence between experiences related in a narrative and the experiences of its recipients. Dubos observed that auditors were much more responsive to descriptions portraying passions and situations familiar to them than to those that were unfamiliar. Because they illuminated the listeners' own experiences, such familiar portrayals seemed more plausible. "We are principally sensitive to the worries and afflictions of those who resemble us in their character," Dubos said. "All discourses that bring us back to ourselves and that support us in our own sentiments have a particular attraction for us."[71/oo] Because of the auditors' tendency to relate what they heard to their own experience, events running counter to their conception of what was possible lacked *vraisemblance;* Dubos observed that the raconteur who changed events or experiences known to the audience would not be believed.[72] What was plausible was linked to what was possible as well as to what was actual; "as truth is the soul of history, *vraisemblance* is the soul of all fiction and all poetry."[73/pp] Orators and writers therefore were required to

---

nn. l'historien qui a un vrai génie choisit sur vingt endroits celui où un fait sera mieux placé pour répandre la lumière sur tous les autres. Souvent un fait montré par avance de loin débrouille tout ce qui le prépare. Souvent un autre sera mieux dans son jour étant mis en arrière. En présentant plus tard, il viendra plus à propos pour faire naître d'autres événements.

oo. nous sommes sensibles principalement aux inquiétudes comme aux afflictions de ceux qui nous ressemblent par leur caractere. Tous les discours qui nous ramenent à nous mêmes, & qui nous entretiennent de nos propres sentimens, ont pour nous un attrait particulier.

pp. comme la verité est l'ame de l'histoire, la vraisemblance est l'ame de toute fiction & de toute Poësie.

construct narratives that conformed to their audiences' conceptions of what was possible. Failure to do so would undermine the credibility of their accounts, much like the appearance of fallacious reasoning undermines the cogency and credibility of arguments.

Clarity

French concern for clarity had its origins partly in Descartes' insistence upon clear and distinct ideas. In their *La Logique, ou l'art de penser,* Antoine Arnauld and Pierre Nicole had noted that an idea is clear when one knows everything to which it can be applied and distinct when one knows everything that can be included within it.[74] The Port Royalists applied standards of clarity and distinctness when they discussed equivocation, ambiguous language, and other abuses leading to obscurity of thought. Lamy followed a similar pattern of thought in reminding his readers that what was said should be carefully proportioned to reflect the major features of the thought expressed: "Those speak clearly who speak simply, and who express their thoughts in a natural manner in the same order and extent that they are in their minds."[75/qq]

The strict correspondence of language to thought was emphasized also by Bouhours who held that words represented thoughts one-to-one. Obscurity and falseness thus resulted from a mismatch between the terms used and the reality they described. "Thoughts . . . are the images of things, as words are the images of thoughts; and to think . . . is to form in oneself the painting of a spiritual or sensible object. However, images and paintings are only true insofar as they are likenesses: thus a thought is true when it represents things faithfully; and it is false when it makes them appear other than they are in themselves."[76/rr] Thus speech that functioned like a mirror present-

---

qq. Ceux-là parlent clairement qui parlent simplement, qui expriment leurs pensées d'une manière naturelle, dans le même ordre, dans le même étendue qu'elles sont dans leur esprit.

rr. Les pensées . . . sont les images des choses, comme les paroles sont les images des pensées; & penser . . . c'est former en soy la peinture d'un objet ou spirituel ou sensible. Or les images & les peintures ne sont véritables qu'autant qu'elles sont resemblantes: ainsi une pensée est vraye lors qu'elle représente les choses fidellement; & elle est fausse quand elle les fait voir autrement qu'elles ne sont en elles-mesmes.

ing a strictly correspondent image of thought was regarded as "true" speech.

Bouhours' representational view emerged in his metaphor of a clear thought resembling a light that attracts attention and illuminates its surroundings. This illumination enabled immediate and effortless understanding on the part of the audience. "It is necessary . . . that a thought be so clear, that the readers or hearers understand it effortlessly: that is, it must enter their minds like light enters their eyes without their thinking about it, in such a way that the concern should not be to be understood but for it to be impossible not to be understood."[77/ss] Bouhours' thinking here established a principle stressed in all belletristic rhetorics—clarity was a sine qua non of persuasive communication. No matter how elegant or figured a passage, it will fail to communicate if it is not understood. Understanding must be facilitated by the writer or orator in every way possible. Obscurity and confusion must be avoided, because the listener or reader who cannot follow or understand what a speaker says will be fatigued and thereby unaffected.

Fénelon succinctly reminded his readers that "an author must not leave anything to be sought in his thoughts."[78/tt] The author's first and principal care must be to be understood: "One should never take two steps at a time and should stop to see if he is followed by the multitude. Singularity . . . is dangerous in everything.[79/uu] As Bouhours observed, lack of clarity often resulted from a speaker's own confusion, as well as from digressions, irrelevant thoughts, misapplied metaphors, and comparisons that had no rapport with the thought expressed.[80] Overcompressed thoughts, wherein a speaker failed adequately to develop ideas, could also lead to confusion.[81]

Communicators who succeeded at perspicuous self-expression might find their success unrecognized and unappreciated.

---

ss. Il faut . . . qu'une pensée soit si claire, que les Lecteurs ou les Auditeurs l'entendent sans qu'ils s'appliquent à la concevoir: c'est-à-dire, qu'elle entre dans leur esprit comme la lumiére entre dans leurs yeux lors qu'ils n'y font pas de réflexion; de sorte que le soin de celuy qui pense, doit estre non que sa pensée puisse s'entendre, mais qu'elle ne puisse ne s'entendre pas.

tt. Un auteur ne doit laisser rien à chercher dans sa pensée.

uu. On ne doit jamais faire deux pas à la fois et il faut s'arrêter dès qu'on ne se voit pas suivi de la multitude. La singularité est dangereuse en tout.

Rollin observed that "when one reads or hears discourse of this kind, the least eloquent believe themselves capable of imitating it. They believe that, but they are mistaken; and to be convinced, one must only try: for after many efforts, one will often be forced to admit that one was unable to succeed."[82/vv] Rollin's mention here of seeming effortlessness was a common *topos* of the belletrists because they viewed an audience's awareness of a speaker's artfulness as undesirable. Lamy's concept of *l'adresse* was here developed in the idea that a speaker's or writer's art must be unobtrusive and apparently natural.

Conclusion

The rhetorical theories of French belletrists eventuated in a transformation of the nature and *telos* of rhetorical theory. The neoclassical preoccupation with production of discourse shifted to interest in modes of reception. Lamy, Bouhours, Fénelon, Rollin, and Dubos were principally interested in predispositions, habits of mind, cultural conventions, and other factors that caused audiences to experience certain discursive elements as appropriate and natural. The psychological makeup of audiences was emphasized in Lamy's theory of *l'adresse* or insinuation, Dubos' "sixth sense," and Bouhours' preoccupation with attentiveness. Such agendas were compatible with the faculty psychology and introspective empiricism of the Sottish belletrists. Elements of French belletrism could thus be extended and adapted to Adam Smith's views on sympathy, Humean and commonsense theories of taste, George Campbell's conception of *vraisemblance* and plausibility, and the Scots' general emphasis upon perspicuity and vivacity as means of arousing and sustaining attention.

Further, eighteenth-century belletrism acquired and developed aesthetics by applying it to the forms and categories of cognitive response. Merging the discursive genres of oratory, poetry, history, and literature, the French belletrists empha-

---

vv. quand on lit ou qu'on entend un discours de ce genre, les moins éloquens se croient capables de l'imiter. On le croit, mais on se trompe; et pour s'en convaincre, il ne faut qu'en faire l'essai: car après bien des efforts, on sera contraint souvent d'avouer qu'on n'a pas pu y parvenir.

sized proportion, simplicity, and artfulness of imitation. Discourse possessing such elements was said to be "natural," "true," and thus affecting. Scottish belletrists pursued this interest by developing specific theories of the Sublime, the beautiful, and the picturesque. But there were special problems to be solved. Did aesthetic pleasure arise from the nature of the object, the character of emotional response, or the artfulness of the portrayal? What was the relationship of style to aesthetic beauty? How did aesthetic qualities operate upon the various faculties to incite response? Prodigious effort by the major theorists of the age was invested in answering such questions. The origins of such issues in French rhetorics and their eventual development in the late eighteenth century will be the focus of chapters 2, 3, and 4.

Chapter 2

Propriety

In late seventeenth-century France, a few theoretically significant critical terms formed a conceptual web of critical theory. Such terms as *bienséance, convenance, vraisemblance, raison,* and *nature* had very different meanings then than they do now. *Raison,* for example, did not refer to formal reasoning or to informal logic. Instead, it referred to an intrinsic understanding or discernment, a faculty of intuitively distinguishing good from bad and false from true.[1] And, the *nature* to which so many critics alluded was not related to the natural world but to a nature reformed and purified by art, idealization, order, and symmetry. Likewise, *bienséance, convenance,* and *vraisemblance* possessed specialized meanings growing out of French classicism's motive to reform human sensibility and art on the model of the ancient classics.

In his use of these critical terms, Fénelon's views were representative of his time and of the French classicists. In particular, the theme of *bienséance,* or propriety, is threaded throughout his literary and rhetorical theories as articulated in his *Dialogues sur l'éloquence* and his *Lettre à l'Académie.*[2] In his analysis of Fénelon, François Varillon speaks of the "desperate nostalgia for unity" in the Fénelonian aesthetic.[3] An insistence upon propriety, order, coherence, simplicity, and artlessness recurred in Fénelon's views on style, presentation, arrangement, and characterization in poetry, drama, oratory, and other forms of prose. The significance of *bienséance* in Fénelon's theory and in the theories that followed it should be appreciated in light of the original meaning of the term in the seventeenth-century intellectual and cultural milieu.

Bienséance and Other Critical Terms

Bienséance as an aesthetic term has its origins in social practices, and its etymology is best understood in this light. Used in the plural, *les bienséances* referred to social conventions and tacit rules as to what was appropriate in a given social situation. Those who observed *les bienséances* knew from experience how to adjust their conduct to the parties present and to other situational constraints. *Les bienséances* originated among the court nobility and, in the hierarchical society of late seventeenth-century France everyone was eager to observe them, for proper knowledge and use of such conventions were a sign of an individual's membership in an elite social class. Books such as le chevalier de Méré's *De la conversation* counseled readers on proper observance of *les bienséances*—when to speak, when to remain silent, how to address persons of superior rank, what subjects to avoid, how to change the subject, and how to provide an appropriate transition.[4] Provincial nobility, urban tradesmen, and others read such books avidly and sought to emulate the practices of the *honnête homme. Les bienséances,* taken together, comprised *la bienséance,* a regulative concept in social life.

In the aesthetic sphere, *bienséance* also had a regulative function. In drama and poetry, it referred to whether characters acted in conformity with the social conventions and practices indigenous to their culture, station, and era, and to whether their conduct and speech suited the taste of the day and the expectations of the audience. Volume 1 of the Robert dictionary defines the French classicists' conception of *bienséance* as a "quality by which a work respects the canonical forms particular to its epoch and responds exactly, in its genre, to the standards of taste."[5/a] *Bienséance* had two dimensions—internal and external. Internal application was concerned with whether a character's actions conformed to his rank, profession, age, and situation. In other words, did the character's conduct conform to his ideal type? External application was concerned with whether a depiction conformed to the audience's expectation of what was normal, appropriate, and suited to its taste.[6] A critic seeking to apply *bienséance* in judging discourse and literature, then, would ask whether the behaviors

---

a. Qualité par laquelle une oeuvre respecte les formes canoniques particulières à son époque et répond exactement, dans son genre, aux critères du goût.

of the portrayed persons conformed to their types and to audience expectations of how those types should normally behave.

An author's consistent observation of *bienséance* in his work meant that it would have *convenance*—agreement, seemliness, decorum. *Bienséance* and *convenance* were closely related in that the first was constitutive of the second. Jean Mesnard observed that "in the expression of ideas, to obtain *la convenance* with human nature is nothing other than to seek after what pleases and to avoid what displeases. It is, after all, to respect strictly *les bienséances*."[7/b] A third concept highly related to these was *la vraisemblance,* or verisimilitude. Like the other two concepts, *vraisemblance* grew out of a general notion of what was natural and appropriate in a given circumstance. Boileau made this point well when he observed that: "Le vrai n'est quelquefois pas vraisembable."[8] By this, Boileau meant that *vraisemblance* was not related to truth in an empirical or metaphysical sense (i.e., that which corresponds to sense data or to a divine truth). Rather, it corresponds to regularities and paradigms of human action and behavior. An action might be "true" (might have occurred) and yet lack *vraisemblance* because of its monstrous or aberrant nature.

Unlike *bienséance,* which was manifest in particular situations, *vraisemblance* was a generalized phenomenon. A. Kibédi Varga identified three dimensions of *vraisemblance* in French classicism—moral, philosophical, and social. In its moral sense, *vraisemblance* aimed to improve mores by depicting things as they ought to be. In its philosophical sense, it universalized human action and left "to the reader the effort of abstracting the particular, of seizing the general sense of the fable."[9/c] In its social sense, *vraisemblance* humanized history and rendered comprehensible bare facts and actions whose meaning would otherwise escape us. An account or portrayal possessing *vraisemblance* was aesthetically satisfying because it seemed natural; it gave the reader or listener a sense of recognition, familiarity, and ease.[10]

---

b. Dans l'expression des idées, obtenir la convenance avec la nature humaine n'est encore autre chose que de rechercher ce qui plaît et de fuir ce qui déplaît. C'est, en définitive, respecter strictement les bienséances.

c. permet au lecteur l'effort de faire abstraction du particulier, de saisir le sens général de la fable.

In aesthetic and critical circles of the seventeenth and eighteenth centuries, terms such as these were central. Despite the efforts of Boileau and others to articulate rules or guidelines for art, aesthetic judgment remained a function of the *je ne sais quoi,* the individual's ability to distinguish the good from the bad and to apply *la raison*—discernment or good sense—to works of discourse or of art. This is very much the case in Fénelon's theories, since he valued unobtrusiveness and artlessness. Any dimension of a work that would call attention to its author was abjured. Overworked style, rhyming, caricature, intrigue, and diversion all were to be avoided. To combat self-consciousness in art, Fénelon recommended observance of propriety, proportion, and coherence. Of his work, E. B. O. Borgerhoff observed that "the emphasis is always on attractiveness, on hidden order as opposed to division. . . ."[11] Considering the applications of *bienséance* in Fénelon's rhetorical theory will enable us to appreciate the applications and extensions made of this concept in later belletristic theories of rhetoric.

Bienséance in Fénelon's Rhetorical Theory

The value placed on order and unity by Fénelon was manifest in many of his positions on the critical issues of his day. He objected to rhyme in poetry because it forced the poet to add superfluous phrases to fill out the cadence and meter. He criticized Gothic architecture because he found its "windows, roses, and little knacks" gauche and displeasing.[12] In art, he preferred Raphaël and Poussin for their harmony and idealization of nature.[13] As Jeanne-Lydie Goré explained, "Fénelon experiences a sort of recoil against the modern taste for the rare and original. . . . He is persuaded that all men have in them an instinct that does not mislead them. . . ."[14/d] In Fénelon's view, a work that evinced unity, coherence, and good sense ought to appeal naturally to its audience's taste for order and harmony.

In regard to eloquence, Fénelon's emphasis on propriety and coherence meant that style should be suited to the matter

---

d. Fénelon éprouve une sorte de recul devant le goût moderne du rare et de l'original. . . . Il est persuadé que tous les hommes ont en eux un instinct qui ne les trompe pas. . . .

treated, that arrangement should not be imposed but should suit the configuration of the subject, and that the speaker should suit his delivery to the emotional pitch and importance of his topic. Fénelon distrusted persuasive strategies; he disliked Aristotle's *Rhetoric* because it contained "many dry precepts—precepts which are more curious than useful in practice."[15/e] Instead, he preferred the works of St. Augustine and the pseudo-Longinus. St. Augustine shared Fénelon's preoccupation with religious eloquence and with speaking to the converted, while the treatise *On the Sublime* emphasized the emotive rather than the presentational dimensions of speaking. Fénelon believed that people were moved more by great conceptions and vehement passion than by rhetorical devices, and he agreed wholeheartedly with the Longinian tenet that "art is perfect when it seems to be nature, and nature hits the mark when she contains art hidden within her."[16] Fénelon also preferred these treatises because they instructed their readers through examples rather than through instructions and precepts.

Fénelon's rhetorical theory was unusual in its view of eloquence as a form of portraiture. As I noted in chapter 1, the *Dialogues* and the *Lettre* often compare the orator to a painter. The metaphor of the visible occurred frequently in Fénelon's descriptions of an orator's art. "The true orator," he said, "adorns his speech with luminous truths," and he threads his central thesis throughout his work "in much the same way [as] a painter paints his painting so that light emanates naturally from a single source to each object."[17/f] Wilbur S. Howell, who considered the theme of portraiture in Fénelon's rhetorical theory, noted that in the *Dialogues* genuine persuasion required that men's passions be stirred; only where strong feelings were engaged could the auditor be moved. "To prove . . . is to convince the auditor that a proposition is true. . . . To excite strong feelings is to be forced to do two things beyond proof: to portray and to strike."[18] To portray was to paint with words through

---

e. . . . beaucoup de préceptes secs, et plus curieux qu'utiles dans la pratique.

f. Le véritable orateur n'orne son discours que de véritez lumineuses . . . de même qu'un peintre place dans son tableau le jour en sorte que d'un seul endroit il distribue à chaque objet son degré de lumière.

vivid description and lively images. Fénelon described it in this way:

> To portray is not only to describe things but to represent their surrounding features in so lively and so concrete a way that the listener imagines himself almost seeing them. . . . A simple story cannot move. It is necessary not only to acquaint listeners with the facts, but to make the facts visible to them, and to strike their consciousness by means of a perfect representation of the arresting manner in which the facts have come to pass. . . . If one does not have this genius to portray, never can one impress things upon the soul of the listener—all is dry, flat, boring. Since the time of the original sin, man has been entirely enmeshed in palpable things. . . . He cannot long be attentive to that which is abstract. It is necessary to give a physical body to all the instructions one wishes to inject into his soul. It is necessary to have images to beguile him.[19/g]

Fénelon's union of portraiture with persuasion suggested the impossibility of divorcing aesthetics from rhetoric.[20] If oratory is seen as portraiture, aesthetic criteria such as proportion, harmony, and symmetry can be applied to eloquence. With portraiture and depiction in discourse as starting points, *bienséance* becomes a useful way of making aesthetic standards concrete. It implies that the form of expression should be internally coherent and should suit the character of the subject and the speaker. Fénelon's inclination to thematize propriety in his discussions of style, presentation, and arrangement thus fit well with his general aesthetic position and his view of how oratory ought to function.

---

g. Peindre, c'est non-seulement décrire les choses, mais en représenter les circonstances d'une manière si vive et si sensible, que l'auditeur s'imagine presque les voir. . . . Un récit simple ne peut émouvoir: il faut non-seulement instruire les auditeurs des faits, mais les leur rendre sensibles, et frapper leurs sens par une représentation parfaite de la manière touchante dont ils sont arrivés. . . . Si on n'a ce génie de peindre, jamais on n'imprime les choses dans l'âme de l'auditeur; tout est sec, languissant et ennuyeux. Depuis le péché originel, l'homme est tout enfoncé dans les choses sensibles . . . il ne peut être longtemps attentif à ce qui est abstrait. Il faut donner du corps à toutes les instructions qu'on veut insinuer dans son esprit; il faut des images qui l'arrêtent. . . .

With regard to style, the form of expression should be suited to the character and the situation of the person speaking. Fénelon particularly admired the style of Demosthenes' *Philippics*. Demosthenes' use of direct address, rhetorical questions, and a sparse, tightly woven style seemed perfectly suited to the grave situation in which the Athenians found themselves and to the sense of urgency felt by the speaker. Unlike Lamy and other theorists who felt that figures of speech were essential to express passion, Fénelon believed that they were often misplaced in impassioned discourse. "I confess that the florid style has its charms," he said, "but they are misplaced in discourses which do not call for refined witticisms and in which great passions must be expressed."[21/h]

Fénelon was dismayed by his contemporaries' fascination with wit and display. Their use of the florid style revealed no more than their desire to call attention to themselves and to their artistry. In Fénelon's view, floridity was particularly misplaced in sermons and homilies where the speaker sought salvation and moral improvement in his parishioners. "The more an orator tries to dazzle me with the marvels of his discourse, the more I am shocked by his vanity. His eagerness to display his wit seems to make him unworthy of admiration. I seek a serious man who speaks for my sake and not for his own, who seeks my salvation and not his own glorification."[22/i] Consistent use of the high style and of grandiloquence in religious speaking, then, was viewed as inappropriate.

Fénelon's disparagement of figured expression should be contextualized as a reaction to the excesses of his time, and not as an unequivocal endorsement of the attic style. Dry, unembellished prose might be appropriate for works of philosophy or instruction, but it was ill-suited to oratory. Fénelon made this distinction clear in discussing genres of discourse.

---

h. J'avoue que le genre fleuri a ses grâces; mais elles sont déplacées dans les discours où il ne s'agit point d'un jeu d'esprit plein de délicatesse et où les grandes passions doivent parler.

i. Plus un déclamateur feroit d'efforts pour m'éblouir par les prestiges de son discours, plus je me révolterois contre sa vanité. Son empressement pour faire admirer son esprit me paroîtroit le rendre indigne de toute admiration. Je cherche un homme sérieux qui me parle pour moi et non pour lui, qui veuille mon salut et non sa vaine gloire.

A. But what would you say of a man who establishes truth in an exact, dry, naked way, who puts his arguments in good order or makes use of the method of geometers in his speeches, but who does not add anything figurative? Would he be an orator?

B. No. He would merely be a philosopher.

A. Then, in order to make an orator, we must choose a philosopher, that is, a man who knows how to establish the truth; and we must add to the exactitude of his arguments the beauty and vehemence of living discourse if we would make an orator of him.[23/j]

Like St. Augustine, Fénelon rejected ornamentation for its own sake but still believed in the importance of varying styles, using figures, and enlivening substance in order to achieve attentiveness and persuasion in listeners. What was essential was to suit the style to the matter rather than to embellish indiscriminately thoughts and appeals that did not call for embellishment. The plain style should be used to instruct and inform, the middle style to hold attention and to persuade, and the high style to captivate and impassion listeners. The styles should be varied with the speaker's topic and purpose and should always be formed with a eye to *bienséance*. In his *Lettre*, Fénelon concluded his discussion of style by saying "there is a propriety to be observed with words as with clothes. A grieving widow does not wear mourning clothes with embroidery, frills, and ribbons. An apostolic missionary should not make a vain, affected utterance of the word of God."[24/k]

This emphasis on proportion was equally apparent in

---

j. A. Mais que diriez-vous d'un homme qui prouveroit la vérité d'une manière exacte, sèche, nue, qui mettroit ses arguments en bonne forme, ou qui se serviroit de la méthode de géomètres dans ses discours publics, sans y ajouter rien de vif et de figuré? Seroit-ce un orateur?

B. Non, ce ne seroit qu'un philosophe.

A. Il faut donc, pour faire un orateur, choisir un philosophe, c'est-à-dire un homme qui sache prouver la vérité, et ajouter à l'exactitude de ses raisonnements la beauté et la véhémence d'un discours varié, pour en faire un orateur.

k. Il y a une bienséance à garder pour les paroles comme pour les habits. Une veuve désolée ne porte point le deuil avec beaucoup de broderie, de frisure et de rubans. Une missionnaire apostolique ne doit point faire de la parole de Dieu une parole vaine et pleine d'ornemens affectez.

Fénelon's views on arrangement. He disagreed with the then-current practice of apportioning sermons into preset divisions. Noting that such divisions introduced an order "more apparent than real," Fénelon viewed them as an actual hindrance to effective communication. "No longer is there genuine unity— there are two or three distinct discourses unified only by arbitrary interconnection. Day-before-yesterday's sermon, yesterday's sermon, and today's sermon . . . make as much of a unity and a living whole together as the three points of one of these sermons make when they are put together."[25/l] Divisions such as this were inappropriate because they were imposed. Since they did not arise from the nature of the matter treated, they disrupted a discourse's natural order and coherence. Fénelon recommended instead an arrangement in accordance with the "actual connection of things."[26/m] "When you divide, it is necessary to divide simply, naturally. One must have a division that is found ready-made in the very subject itself; a division that clarifies, that puts material into classes, that is easily remembered, and that helps one to retain everything else; a division, in short, that reveals the size of the subject and of its parts."[27/n]

Effective arrangement comes not from predictable divisions, prefatory partitioning, or obvious signposts. Rather, it arises from an orator's instinctive understanding of the significance of various parts of his subject and the capacities of his audience. An abstruse yet vital point may require frequent restatement; sometimes a chain of ideas leads inevitably to a conclusion; a series of events may need to be introduced by the history and traditions that precede them.[28] Implicit in the configuration of the subject is the pattern of arrangement best

---

l. Il n'y a plus d'unité véritable, ce sont deux ou trois discours différents qui ne sont unis que par une liaison arbitraire. Le sermon d'avant-hier, celui d'hier et celui d'aujourd'hui . . . font autant ensemble un tout et un corps de discours, que les trois points de ces sermons font un tout entre eux.

m. la véritable liaison des matières

n. Quand on divise, il faut diviser simplement, naturellement. Il faut que ce soit une division qui se trouve toute faite dans le sujet même; une division qui éclaircisse, qui range les matières, qui se retiene aisément, et qui aide à retenir tout le reste; enfin une division qui fasse voir la grandeur du sujet et de ses parties.

suited to it. Propriety consists in discovering this pattern and using it to communicate to listeners a clear and distinct idea of the speaker's thesis.

In delivery, Fénelon recommended the same sort of connection between the substance of a speech and the physical and vocal manner of presenting it. He said that "the movement of the body is . . . a painting of the thoughts of the soul."[29/o] In his posture, gestures, demeanor, and inflection, a speaker should seek to project the feelings natural to the matter and situation. Fénelon made this most apparent when he considered the speaker whose actions were inappropriate: "His body must have movement when his words have movement, and his body must stand moveless when his words are calm and simple. Nothing seems to me so shocking and absurd as to see a man whip himself into a fury in order to tell me something dispassionate."[30/p] Fénelon then recounted an instance in which a preacher "lash[ed] himself in a extraordinary way" while merely announcing the topic upon which he would preach the following Sunday. The mismatch between the man's manner and his matter gave a ludicrous effect. Anything other than seemingly natural behavior would call attention to itself and undermine the speaker's purpose, which ought to be the instruction and moral improvement of his listeners.

In Fénelon's theory, then, propriety was conceived as a proportionate correspondence between *fond* and *forme,* between the structure and substance of the subject and the manner in which it was expressed. For all the discursive arts—poetry, drama, and history, as well as oratory—Fénelon insisted upon propriety. He criticized preachers for selecting scripture ill-suited to the sermonic message, playwrights for introducing amorous intrigue into tragedy, and historians for describing customs and mores nonexistent in a particular era.[31]

Not only were such practices unnatural and affected, they misled and distracted audiences. Discourse in which *bienséance* was observed would seem effortless and unaffected. Such

---

o. Le mouvement du corps est . . . une peinture des pensées de l'âme.

p. Il faut que son corps ait du mouvement quand ses paroles en ont, et que son corps demeure tranquille quand ses paroles n'ont rien que de doux et de simple. Rien ne me semble si choquant et si absurde, que de voir un homme qui se tourmente pour me dire des choses froides.

discourse engendered "a sublime so familiar, gentle, and simple that at first everyone believes he could have easily found it himself although few are capable of it."[32/q] *Bienséance* was thus an aesthetic property of eloquence that had a rhetorical effect. Like the symmetry and proportion in the paintings of Poussin, coherence, balance, and naturalness in speech would evoke admiration and an affective response from listeners.

Fénelon's theory sought an intuitive and aesthetic response rather than one that was purely rational. Listeners were to be engaged rather than convinced, or more appropriately, captivated and struck by the features of discourse so as to be convinced. Fénelon viewed proportion and correspondence between the substance and circumstances of a discourse and the manner of its expression as essential. He felt that facility in rhetorical expression was to be acquired through the study of fine examples rather than through learning rules and principles. These features of his theory were especially appealing to his successors in the Scottish Enlightenment as they sought to develop their own belletristic theories of rhetoric, and I turn now to those influences.

Sympathy and Propriety in Adam Smith's *Lectures*

Adam Smith was probably quite familiar with Fénelon's works on rhetoric, although there is no direct manuscript evidence that he had read them. As I noted in the introduction, posterity's only record of Smith's *Lectures on Rhetoric and Belles Lettres* is an imperfect manuscript of student copyists' notes, first published by John Lothian in 1963.[33] Prior to his death in 1790, Smith had ordered his own manuscript copy of his lectures destroyed.[34] Even if Smith had cited Fénelon's works (and it is very likely that he did), contemporary readers would be unable to ascertain the location or extent of citations because nearly all the names of French authors in the extant manuscript are either omitted or distorted.[35]

---

q. un sublime si familier, si doux et si simple que chacun soit d'abord tenté de croire qu'il l'auroit trouvé sans peine, quoique peu d'hommes soient capables de le trouver.

Many of Smith's orientations and prejudices were similar to Fénelon's. Both men were concerned with literate expression in all the discursive arts—history, literature, eloquence, and didactic writing. Both explicitly valued unobtrusiveness in art and expression and believed that speakers and writers should form their thoughts in a manner natural, coherent, and suited to the capacities of their audiences. "A natural order of expression," Smith observed, "consists in what we call easy writing which makes the sense of the author flow naturally upon our mind without our being obliged to hunt backwards and forwards in order to find it."[36] This insistence upon sparing the reader and avoiding distraction is quite reminiscent of what Fénelon had to say on the same subject.

Nowhere do the two theorists coincide more closely than in their views on propriety. Their reasons for valuing propriety differed, however. Fénelon possessed a fundamentally classicist love for uniformity and order. In his view, the author who struck a balance between *forme* and *fond* and who evinced instinctive awareness of the social mores and aesthetic proclivities of his audience would appeal to a universal affection for what seemed orderly and suitable. Smith, influenced by associationist psychology and eighteenth-century empiricism, had a more particularized conception of propriety. He believed that its observance enabled a writer or orator to appeal to his hearers *by sympathy*.[37]

Smith defined sympathy as a "fellow-feeling" with any passion experienced by another person. Through an empathic understanding of what the other person experienced, a reader or audience would come to experience something similar. In his *Theory of Moral Sentiments*, Smith described this process: "By the imagination we place ourselves in his situation, we conceive ourselves enduring all the same torments, we enter as it were into his body, and become in some measure the same person with him, and thence form some idea of his sensation and even feel something which, though weaker in degree, is not altogether unlike them."[38] Observance of propriety is key to the workings of sympathy because propriety is what enables listeners to identify with the speaker and the experiences and responses the speaker seeks to promote. If the speaker's expression, intensity, manner, or level of style is not matched

to what listeners themselves would experience in similar circumstances, if the proprieties of behavior and feeling are violated, then the rhetor will have no effect upon his listeners.
Misplaced passion, overblown expression, or unnatural order
will thus cause miscarriage of the rhetor's design. Smith argued for propriety by observing that "in the suitableness or un-
suitableness, in the proportion or disproportion which the
affection seems to bear to the cause or object which excites it,
consists the propriety or impropriety, the decency or ungrace-
fulness of consequent action."[39]

Smith's emphasis on sympathy meant that he was more
concerned with narration as an imitative and re-presentational
act than with argument. He stated his essential view of persuasion when he said that "when the words neatly and properly
expressed the thing to be described, and conveyed the sentiment the author entertained of it and desired to communicate
by sympathy to his hearers; then the expression had all the
beauty language was capable of bestowing on it."[40] Smith
viewed discourse as essentially reproductive; it should narrate
events as they occurred, leave no gaps, portray characters true
to life, avoid digression, connect causes to events, and include
only what was relevant.[41] Rather than attending to the mechanisms of proof, Smith devoted most of his *Lectures* to articulat-
ing the principles of appropriate and suitable exposition and
narration.

One of Smith's editors, J. C. Bryce, has commented on
Smith's neglect of the inventional devices of scholastic rhetoric:
"He often shows his impatience with the intricate subdivisions
and classifications of his subject. . . . The orator's art had long
been divided into invention, arrangement, expression, memory,
and delivery. . . . Smith in effect sees only the second and third
as important, the third (style) occupying Lectures 2–11, and
the second underlying virtually all that lectures 12–30 discuss."[42] In discussing the discursive genres, Smith in fact devoted five lectures (12–16) to description, four (17–20) to
narration and historical writing, one (21) to poetry, two (22–
23) to panegyric, one (24) to didactic, three (25–27) to deliberative, and three (28–30) to judicial or forensic oratory. When
he finally approached the question of proofs in his twenty-fifth
lecture, Smith wasted no time in noting how unnecessary was

detailed study of argument: "The arguments that are to be used before a people cannot be very intricate; the Proposition generally requires no proof at all and when it does the arguments are of themselves so evident as not to require any elaborate explanation. . . . As the arguments are in themselves so simple, there can be no great nicety required in the arrangement. And in general in every sort of eloquence the choice of the arguments and the proper arrangement of them is the least difficult matter."[43] In Smith's last six lectures, he gave very little attention to proof, nor did he believe such attention was necessary, since the rules he had earlier given on narrative composition could "with a few alterations" apply equally well to discourse in which the author aimed to prove a proposition or a series of propositions.

Although we cannot establish a direct linkage, Smith emulated Fénelon in treating discourse as a painting or portrayal of the objects it represented. The quality of a discourse could therefore be judged according to its fidelity and coherence. Portraiture was one of the three requisite qualities of fine composition as Smith listed them: "1st—That [the writer] have a complete knowledge of his Subjects; 2dly That he should arrange all the parts of his Subject in their proper order; 3dly That he paint ⟨or⟩ describe the Ideas he has of these severall in the most proper and expressive manner; this is the art of painting or imitation. . . ."[44] This painting "in the most proper and expressive manner" consisted largely in observing the tacit conventions of propriety. In Smith's view, a discourse's style should suit the emotions expressed, the objects described, the author's circumstances and humor, and the audience's capacities. Writers such as Addison and Swift who observed these conventions were praised by Smith; others who neglected them were generally criticized.

In expressing emotion, Smith viewed figures of speech as unnecessary and often inapt. "It matters not," Smith observed, "whether the figures of speech are introduced. . . ."[45] Instead, he viewed the cadence of expression as important; joy and grief should "burst out into periods," whereas anger and indignation should be expressed in a broken, irregular manner.[46] Whereas admiration would be expressed in superlatives, love called for simple, natural speech and the avoidance of magnifying expressions. Voicing sentiments in a way conforming to experience thus increased the intrinsic appeal of discourse.

Smith also believed that descriptions should be so configured as to correspond to what they described. Events should be ordered as they occurred, and similar objects should be grouped together while disparate ones were kept apart. Important matters should be attended to and trivial ones ignored. Smith criticized the historian Clarendon for dwelling on insignificant events and extensively describing characters of minor importance.[47]

Smith was more explicit than his French predecessors in arguing that an author's style and manner of expression should suit his humor and circumstances. Even though Jonathan Swift's style was harsh and unpleasant, Smith viewed it as appropriate because it suited Swift's morose humor.[48] Likewise, Demosthenes' familiar, severe, and nervous style was considered appropriate to the high-pitched, unfeeling nature of the man. Smith believed that speakers and the people they described should act in character. "A gay man should not endeavor to be grave nor the grave man to be gay, but each should regulate that character and manner . . . and hinder it from running into that vicious extreme to which he is most inclined."[49] Smith sought for a mean in self-expression, a mean that arose from the character of the author himself.

The dimensions and form of discourse should suit the natural capacities and expectations of its audience. On this topic Smith shared Fénelon's spirit but was more detailed. Smith noted that primitive people appreciate wondrous and fabulous accounts, whereas enlightened and cultivated auditors require greater subtlety and refinement.[50] He recommended the Aristotelian method for audiences favoring a speaker's thesis and the Socratic method for those negatively predisposed.[51] Propriety also could also be preserved in the manner of speaking; those equal in status to the speaker were to be addressed differently than superiors.[52] Such predispositions and conventions should be kept in mind, for, as Smith noted, "the mind naturally conceives the facts . . . when they are . . . suited to our natural conceptions [and] by that means rendered more distinct."[53]

In Smith's theory of rhetoric, propriety was generally conceived as "suitability" or proportion, and it had an artful dimension. Exactly reproducing something in the medium where it originated was not considered art. Art consisted in making "a thing of one kind resemble another thing of a very different kind."[54] Smith viewed eloquence itself as a medium—one where ideas are represented, events described, and emotions expressed. Artfulness in composition and in self-expression thus consisted of correspondently reproducing the original nature of a matter in the manner of its expression.

Smith resembled Fénelon and other French critics in his emphasis on the aesthetic appeal of discourse. Regardless of the genre in question (poetic, didactic, or rhetorical) Smith, like Fénelon, believed that expression should be natural not overworked, ordered so as to best display connections between events and their causes, and stated so as to best express the author's character and emotions. Smith's efforts to lay out the implications of these principles as applied to description, narration, poetry, and epideictic were reminiscent of Fénelon's consideration of the various genres in his *Letter to the French Academy,* and they made way for the broadened consideration of the discursive arts that we find in later belletristic rhetorics.

Propriety and Plausibility in George Campbell's Works

In recommending rhetorical treatises to his students, George Campbell singled out a very select few. His *Lectures on Pulpit Eloquence* endorsed, among the moderns, only Charles Rollin, François Fénelon, and Hugh Blair.[55] That two of these three men should be French is not surprising when one considers Campbell's thorough familiarity with the French language and with French authors. In his critiques of English language and syntax, Campbell drew more frequently from French than from any other foreign language in making comparisons. In his *Philosophy of Rhetoric,* Campbell cited fifteen contemporary French theorists, among them, Dubos, Bouhours, Rollin, and Boileau.[56]

Fénelon's direct influence on Campbell was more apparent in the latter's remarks on language than in his comments on style and rhetorical affect. Campbell apparently made use of

Fénelon's observations on the impoverishment of the French language, the superiority of Greek and Latin for capturing meter, and the practice of borrowing or adapting words from one language to another.[57] In addition, there are similarities in the two authors' views on eloquence. Both believed that the orator's art should be unobtrusive, that speakers should follow the natural order suggested by their subject matter, and that the best form of oratorical preparation was extensive study improved by practice.[58] Both also valued the naturalness and perspicuity that enabled preachers to focus their parishioners' attention on the substance of the sermonic message and on their own moral improvement.

Considering that both Fénelon's *Dialogues* and Campbell's *Lectures* were written for the same purpose (to improve pulpit eloquence) and for essentially the same kind of audience (practicing and aspiring preachers), the difference between the two is what is most striking. To some extent, this contrast is due to the very different intellectual milieux in which the two men worked—Fénelon in the twilight of French Classicism prior to empiricism and Campbell in the Scottish Enlightenment. Some of the differences are attributable, too, to the very different speaking traditions in Catholic France and Presbyterian Scotland. To a large extent, however, the contrast in their works grew out of the very different intellectual constitutions of the two men.

Fénelon wrote out of a genuine concern to reform the pulpit speaking practices of his day. Through the use of classical models and vivid example, he sought to persuade his readers to eschew floridity and stylistic excess. His aims were thus hortatory—to persuade his readers to reform their speaking practices. Campbell, on the other hand, was a fine analyst and systematizer. His purposes were definitional and instructive—to identify the major types of sermons (explanatory, controversial, commendatory, pathetic, and persuasive) and to delineate the modes of organization and style appropriate to each type. Whereas Fénelon drew upon Platonic and Augustinian conceptions of an ideal discourse aimed at moral reform of the audience, Campbell sought to analyze, define, and explain the workings of various discursive genres for his students.

These differences in procedure and emphasis were reflected in the theorists' treatments of propriety as a rhetorical concept. For Fénelon (and for Smith), propriety or *bienséance* was a global and overarching concept. In their theories, discourse was intended essentially to reproduce or duplicate the matter it conveyed. Observance of propriety preserved the coherence of discourse and ensured its plausibility. Suiting style to substance, organization to content, and delivery to the matter at hand made discourse seem natural and unaffected. Fénelon's and Smith's conceptions of propriety thus influenced every dimension of their rhetorics.

In Campbell's works, propriety had a more specific and specialized role, however. Campbell believed the three essential qualities of style to be purity, perspicuity, and vivacity, and propriety was a dimension of the first of these qualities.[59] Purity was related to the grammatical correctness of a discourse and included avoidance of barbarisms, solecisms, and impropriety. Perspicuity consisted of discursive clarity or understandability. Vivacity, much emphasized by Campbell, arose from a discourse's liveliness or capacity to affect the imagination.[60]

In Campbell's view, purity was a minimal standard to which all discourse ought to adhere. A style might have purity and yet be inadequate; it might be languid, inelegant, flat, or unmusical. Campbell's requirement that a sentence be "a just exhibition, according to the rules of language, of the thought intended to be conveyed by it" was thus a basic stylistic requirement, a sine qua non of effective discourse.[61] Although purity did not in itself ensure rhetorical affect, its absence might seriously hamper a rhetor's efforts. Purity was thus a necessary but not a sufficient condition for stylistic adequacy.

In *The Philosophy of Rhetoric*, Campbell gave some attention to each of three means of violating purity. A person employing a barbarism might use an obsolete or new-coined term or an untoward formation of words in current use. Examples of barbarisms of obsolescence would be "behest," "peradventure," and "self-same." New-coined terms might be "delicatesse" for delicacy and "hauteur" for haughtiness. Frivolous innovations included "incumberment" for encumbrance and "eucharisty" for eucharist. Barbarisms thus were words that were not really English words. Solecisms arose from grammatical inaccuracies or faults in syntax. Campbell provided many examples of this sort of error, such as misuse of verb tense and mood, misstated comparisons, and lack of noun/pronoun agreement.

The third fault against purity—impropriety—received the most attention from Campbell. He noted that impropriety involved the use of properly English words in improper contexts. He observed that whereas a barbarism was an offense against etymology and a solecism one against syntax, an impropriety was an offense against lexicography. "The business of the lexicographer is to assign to every word of the language the precise meaning or meanings which use has assigned it."[62] For Campbell, committing improprieties meant that one used words as signs of things to which use had not affixed them. This violation included malapropisms and other, unintentional misapplications of words.

Campbell's discussion of impropriety in *The Philosophy of Rhetoric* abounded with examples, such as using "observation" for observance and "humanly" for humanely. Since he had based his definition of impropriety on standards of good use, however, Campbell was further obliged to discuss the question of use itself and how it was to be judged. Before taking up the question of linguistic purity, Campbell had identified three qualities of good use that could be called upon in judging the legitimacy of particular linguistic practices. They were that use had to be reputable, present, and national. Reputable use was determined by those who were liberally educated and conversant in relevant subjects. It ensured against the sort of corrupt use and misuse of terms practiced among the unlearned. Whereas in some countries, reputable use might be determined by certain social groups (such as the French court), in England and Scotland it was authorized by the writings of celebrated authors.[63] Present use, of course, was regulated by current linguistic practices, and it implied avoidance of obsolete or archaic words and constructions and of terms that were new and faddish.

Campbell opposed national use to regional and provincial use. He felt that for fullest rhetorical effect, Scotticisms or other regional usages ought to be avoided, as should regional dialects in pronunciation. In his *Lectures on Pulpit Eloquence,* Campbell admonished his students: "Acquire a dialect which will make you understood all over the British Empire." To preachers who might feel that they only needed to be intelligible to their parishioners, Campbell observed: "If you attach yourself to a provincial dialect, it is a hundred to one, that many of your words and phrases will be misunderstood in the very neighbouring province, district, or county. And even though they should be intelligible enough, they have a coarseness and vulgarity in them, that cannot fail to make them appear to men of knowledge and taste ridiculous. . . ."[64] Noting that the English idiom and pronunciation were "daily gaining ground" in Scotland, Campbell in his lectures expressed special concern about improving and standardizing the linguistic practices of his students.[65]

Nor was this concern about avoiding provincial speech and Scotticisms peculiar to Campbell. In late eighteenth-century Scotland, literacy was widespread and basic education available even in rural areas.[66] The universities at Edinburgh and Glasgow had increased dramatically in size during the 1700s. As Richard Sher has noted, it was largely in response to a growing need for a comprehensive, thoroughly modern treatment of the English language and its uses that Smith had begun to offer his lectures in 1748. In campaigning for a rhetoric chair for Adam Ferguson in 1756, John Home had argued that "eloquence in the art of speaking is more necessary for a Scotchman than for anybody else as he lies under some disadvantages which Art must remove."[67] Unlike the Scots, the French belletrists of the preceding century had shared with their readers a single standard of linguistic correctness and purity—the conventions practiced by the French court and its nobility. The Scots' desire for acceptance by their English peers caused their concern about being culturally and intellectually disenfranchised by Scotticisms and regional dialects. This concern thus motivated Campbell's extensive analysis of linguistic practices.

In his discussion of language use in the Scottish Enlightenment, Anand C. Chitnis explained this preoccupation with correctness: "Language was clearly an important attribute of social man. . . . The social institutions of the Scottish Enlightenment were highly dependent on social intercourse. . . . It is clear that the study of language and disquisitions upon it relate closely to an important area of eighteenth-century Scottish thought . . . Language was an index of intelligence and reflected human mentality, knowledge, memory, imagination, sensibility."[68] Linguistic propriety ensured by standards of good use, then, enabled a person to maintain social standing and to communicate with colleagues about matters of importance. Recognizing that his Scottish readers earnestly wished to avoid such linguistic faults as obscurity, equivocation, ambiguity, and affectation, Campbell devoted over one-half of *The Philosophy of Rhetoric* to analysis of the details of style.

Aside from propriety in language use, Campbell envisaged another form of propriety related to content, and this he labeled "plausibility." Just as linguistic convention governs linguistic practice, so does social convention govern how events and practices should be ordered and portrayed by the orator. In his discussion of "circumstances that are chiefly instrumental in operating on the passions," Campbell included "plausibility" which he likened to the French conception of *vraisemblance*. Whereas probability was achievable through sound argument and use of the facts, plausibility arose chiefly from the consistency of a narrative and from its appearing natural and feasible.

A discourse possessing plausibility would fit together the circumstances described so that "those which precede may easily introduce those which follow, and those which follow may appear necessarily out of those which precede."[69] Plausibility went beyond the chronological sequencing of events in Campbell's theory, however. He viewed it as arising from any description in which what was portrayed conformed to experience and expectation so as to appeal to the audience's imagination. In *The Philosophy of Rhetoric,* Campbell provided a fine account of the rhetorical effects of plausibility: "Hence it is, that when a number of ideas relating to any fact or event are successively introduced into my mind by a speaker; if the train he deducith coincide with the general current of my experience; if nothing in it thwart those conclusions and anticipations which are become habitual to me, my mind accompanies him with facility, glides along from one idea to another, and admits the whole with pleasure."[70] This description accounts fully for the general rhetorical effectiveness of plausibility. It facilitates favorable responses in an audience because it fulfills anticipations and expectancies and thus offers a kind of pleasurable satisfaction.

Plausibility in Campbell's theory corresponded to *vrai-semblance* in the belletrist rhetorics of Lamy and Fénelon. *Vraisemblance* and plausibility were valued by audiences who were more likely to be influenced by accounts conforming to their expectations of what was normal and natural than by accounts that lacked this quality. In regard to the sixth canon, plausibility and *vraisemblance* constituted the intellective dimension of a work's appeal; it was persuasive because it possessed verisimilitude for the audience addressed. In comparing belletrist with neoclassical rhetorics, one could say that *vrai-semblance*/plausibility replaced the inventional emphasis on formal and informal logic.

In both *The Philosophy of Rhetoric* and his *Lectures on Pulpit Eloquence,* Campbell's principal aim was to describe how style and expression contributed to a discourse's ability to appeal to the various faculties of its hearers. To that end, he provided a detailed account of how purity, perspicuity, and vivacity were to be obtained, and improper use, obscurity, and feeble expression avoided. He cautioned against impropriety, defined as the misuse and misapplication of words, for speakers who wished to maintain purity of style. In regard to the content or substance of discourse, he advised speakers and writers to be attentive to the presumptions and expectations of their audiences. In sum, Campbell viewed improper expression and implausible narrative as potentially definitive hindrances to successful communication.

Propriety in Hugh Blair's *Lectures*

In Blair's work, one returns to a conception of propriety more global and inclusive than Campbell's. In the latter's theory, propriety had had a localized and limited significance. It was a means of avoiding stylistic impurity. Blair considered propriety in this technical sense, but he also incorporated Smith's conception of empathic identification with its emphasis on the aesthetic appeal of propriety. Blair was, of course, familiar with works of Smith and Campbell and also with the writings of the French belletrists. He explicitly noted his indebtedness to Smith when, in writing about style, he acknowledged that "several ideas have been taken from a manuscript treatise on rhetoric, part of which was shown to me, many years ago, by the learned and ingenious Author, Dr. Adam Smith; and which, it is hoped, will be given by him to the public."[71] Blair read Campbell's *Philosophy of Rhetoric* only after he had composed his lectures. Nonetheless, he found some of Campbell's observations about language and pastoral care compatible with his own views and cited them approvingly in four notes appended to his text.[72]

In the remainder of this chapter, I will explore Blair's views on propriety in detail, comparing them with the views of other rhetoricians I have already discussed. Blair repeatedly referred his students to French authors; among them were Rollin, Crévier, and Fénelon. As this dependance suggests, his approach to rhetoric was considerably more taste-oriented than Campbell's. It is not remarkable, then, that he especially admired Fénelon whose *Lettre* and *Dialogues* he saw as "particularly worthy of perusal, as containing . . . the justest ideas on the subject, that are to be met with in any modern critical writer."[73] Blair explicitly cited Fénelon's views four times in his lectures, but Fénelon's influence on Blair seems to exceed what can be documented through explicit citation.[74] Blair echoed Fénelon's preference for Demosthenes over Cicero, his insistence upon unobtrusiveness, his requirements that style be suited to subject and occasion, and his views on the sublime.[75] Often, too, Blair cited the same sources cited by Fénelon and used wording very similar to the French critic's. It seems safe to say that Blair's conception of propriety was influenced by Fénelon's treatment of the subject.

For Blair, style had two essential qualities—perspicuity and precision. The latter quality grew out of Blair's belief that expression of a thought in language should match exactly the thought represented. Words he viewed as copies of ideas, and he argued that "there must always be a very intimate connection between the manner in which every writer employs words, and his manner of thinking. . . ."[76] Writing that violated the criterion of precision might thus be faulty in three ways: it might express an idea other than the one the author intended; it might express the author's idea only partially; or it might express the idea together with something more than the author intended.[77] Certain of the characteristics of style identified by

Blair—diffuse, concise, feeble, and nervous, for example—
lacked precision.[78] The feeble style failed because of its inability to express fully the author's meaning, whereas the diffuse
style included superfluities and references unrelated to the author's meaning. Because of his belief that discourse should
clearly and distinctly express its author's thoughts, Blair was
as insistent upon precision as Campbell was upon vivacity.[79]

Blair's second stylistic quality, perspicuity, was related to
correctness and standards of good use rather than to representation of thought. Perspicuity included purity of language—
avoiding foreign, obsolete, or new-coined words. It also included
propriety, selecting such words "as the best and most established usage has appropriated to those ideas we intend to
express. . . ."[80] Pure expression would avoid Scotticisms, Galli-
cisms, or ungrammatical, irregular expressions, whereas
proper expression would avoid ill-chosen words that violated
the English conventions of good use. Blair's theory thus merged
purity and propriety with perspicuity into a "correctness standard" of expression. In Campbell's theory, these concepts had
been differently ordered with purity governing the correctness
of expression and perspicuity governing its clarity. Campbell's
views on stylistic propriety were much more fully defined, explained, and exemplified than Blair's. *The Philosophy of Rhetoric* devoted fourteen pages to identifying the types and causes
of impropriety, while Blair's *Lectures* committed only two pages
to purity and propriety.[81]

Blair's view of propriety extended beyond its relevance to
style alone and in this respect his viewpoint was similar to
Smith's. In Blair's view, no writing lacking propriety could aspire to beauty or could fully appeal to sentiment. In his "Critical Dissertation on the Poems of Ossian", Blair had said that
"no sentiments can be beautiful without being proper; that is,
suited to the character and situation of those who utter
them."[82] By thus applying propriety to eloquence, Blair identified it with an intuitive sense of what was suitable and appropriate in a given situation. "No one should ever rise to speak in
public, without forming to himself a just and strict idea of what
suits his own age and character; what suits the subject, the
hearers, the place, the occasion; and adjusting the whole train
and manner of his speaking on this idea."[83] Blair viewed good

style as an expression of the natural character of the speaker or author.[84] He believed, too, that ornamentation and arrangement should suit the level and extensiveness of the subject.[85] The subtlety and complexity of the discourse should be determined by the capacity of its audience, since "no man can be called eloquent, who speaks to an assembly on subjects, or in a strain, which none or few of them comprehend."[86] Finally, the choice of figures and manner of speaking should be adjusted to the taste and habits of the host culture; what suited ancient society was no longer appropriate in the eloquence of the modern period.[87]

Blair's global view of propriety rendered discursive quality more a reflection of intelligence, culture, and taste than a consequence of deliberate, strategic choice by a composer. Whereas Campbell emphasized varying strategies that could yield propriety for specific circumstances, Blair tended to define propriety as a general quality that reflected a composer's entire outlook on people and communication in general. While Campbell strove to explain strategies of propriety in "scientific" ways, Blair treated propriety as an outgrowth of cultural and intuitive excellence. Whether or not Blair depended directly on French belletrists as "authorities" on propriety, his viewpoints and reasoning on the subject were unquestionably consistent with theirs, as he himself recognized.

Conclusion

The French classicist conception of *bienséance* was linked to social conventions and tacit principles governing what was appropriate in a given situation. Aesthetically, this translated into expectations of how a work suited its genre, how portrayals suited a narrative's characters, and whether portraitures conformed to the expectations of their audiences. As representative of this view, Fénelon believed that *bienséance* governed the relation between substance and style, natural order and arrangement, and mood and presentation. Fénelon's preference for unobtrusiveness meant that he valued expression that arose naturally from the configuration of its substance. Fénelon's "nature," however, was not one of flora and fauna but one where portrayals and descriptions were coherent and symmetrical. For Fénelon, oratory was, in a sense, portraiture and ought to be judged according to the aesthetic principles of harmony and proportion.

Smith's views of propriety were appreciative of Fénelon's and yet fundamentally different. Fénelon's *bienséance* functioned as a general classicist aesthetic principle enabling favorable response from listeners because of their inherent preference for order and agreement. Smith's conception was more psychological. For him, propriety was closely linked to sympathy, or a person's ability to experience another's feelings through empathic identification. Speakers violating their listeners' expectations and the conventions of what was suitable would interfere with the process of identification and hinder their own persuasiveness. Conversely, speakers who transformed the matters of which they spoke into forms corresponding to the events portrayed and their listeners' experiences would successfully appeal to their hearers by sympathy.

Both Campbell and Blair considered propriety more specifically in relation to stylistic purity. Connected to the conventions of reputable use, propriety for them meant avoidance of malapropisms and other, unintentional misuse of words and syntax. Although both theorists believed that propriety in itself did not ensure rhetorical effectiveness, they both insisted upon its importance in preserving and promoting good English style. In addition, Campbell expanded the French notion of *vraisemblance* into an aesthetic criterion of persuasive affect. He grouped it with other dimensions of persuasive appeal such as proximity, importance, and immediacy of circumstances as a mechanism to increase the "presence" of discourse and thus its capacity for operating on the passions. In Campbell's notion of plausibility we see *vraisemblance* developed into a basic dimension of discursive appeal.

The Scottish belletrists made limited use of their French predecessors in implementing propriety as a technical requirement of correct language use. In Smith's concept of sympathy, Campbell's account of plausibility, and Blair's global notion of propriety as requisite for rhetorical effectiveness, we see the importance of the French notion of *vraisemblance* in later theories. When the Scottish belletrists adopted their managerial view of rhetoric and set aside systematic treatment of logical argument, there remained a theoretical space where invention once had been. To a considerable extent, this space was filled by notions partially derived from *vraisemblance*. For the cogency of argument was substituted the requirement that descriptions, accounts, and narratives conform to audience expectations of what was normal and appropriate. *Vraisemblance* and its derivative concepts thus drew upon aesthetics to provide the sixth canon's intellective dimension.

Chapter 3

The Sublime

In his *Letter to the French Academy,* Fénelon articulated a critical and aesthetic theory to judge production in many genres—poetry, drama, history, and oratory. Fénelon merged neoclassicist insistence on order and clarity with the modernist requirement that discourse appeal to its audience's tastes and proclivities. Fénelon fused neoclassical and modernist standards so effectively that his work was widely applauded by both the ancients and the moderns in the academy.[1] Nicolas Boileau, French critic and theorist, was unable to effect such a synthesis. The rules for poetry propounded in his *Art poétique* failed to coalesce with the modernist taste for creative spontaneity and innovation. In Boileau's *Oeuvres,* these latter elements survive only in the Sublime, a conception that supplied *pathos,* not only for Boileau's theory, but also for later belletristic rhetorics.

The tensions between Boileau's Sublime and his rules for art can best be understood in terms of Ernst Cassirer's account of the stature and subsequent decline of neoclassicism.[2] Like many historians writing on the late seventeenth century, Cassirer begins his narrative with René Descartes. At the time Boileau formed his aesthetic theory, it was believed that art, like logic, mathematics, and physics, could be systematized and tested by the rules of reason. "The further the spirit of Cartesianism spread," Cassirer observed, "the more decisively and confidently it asserted itself, the more forcefully the new law was proclaimed in the realm of aesthetic theory."[3] Descartes had sought directly to intuit and articulate the universal and inviolable laws of nature. His followers sought exactness and indubitability in every field of human enterprise; the foundation was the same for beauty as for truth.

In 1674, Boileau published his *L'Art poétique,* a neoclassical manifesto of the rules of poetic art.[4] *L'Art poétique* articulated the standards and rules for the poetic genres of epic, tragedy, comedy, lyric, and satire. The work sought to state the norms for artistic practice, identify the sources of poetic error, and suggest remedies. Its critical standard was "reason," but for Boileau reason had nothing to do with logic; rather it was an idealized conception of what was generally thought to be normal and proper.[5] Neoclassical conceptions of reason thus were tied to *bienséance* and *vraisemblance*. They were synonymous, too, with nature, a human nature grounded in an idealized state of society. Cassirer concluded that this tendency to equate reason with social practice meant that "unnoticed, decorum . . . superseded nature and convention [superseded] truth."[6] Boileau's was a rationalism based, not on the immutable geometric forms of the Cartesian system, but on the practices of seventeenth-century culture. Neoclassicism's fate was tied to the fortunes of the culture that housed it; with the demise of that culture, so too would the principles of neoclassicism dissipate.

In Cassirer's view, the subsequent work of Dominique Bouhours was intended as an addendum rather than a corrective of what Boileau had done.[7] In opposition to Boileau's correctness, Bouhours valorized sensitivity or *délicatesse,* which startles the mind and imbues it with new impulse and energy.[8] The shift to indeterminacy and to individual experience reached its fruition in Jean Baptiste Dubos whose *Réflexions critiques sur la poésie et sur la peinture* (1719) sought to free the mind from deduction and to make way for facts and sensory perceptions of art.[9] The locus of Dubos' aesthetics was the taste of the individual percipient, not the rules of a system. The immediate impression an artifact makes, its effect, becomes the focus of Dubos' treatise. A place was thus made for changing forms and varieties of art and for variegated aesthetic experience. Thus, as Cassirer observed, Dubos was "the first to establish introspection as the specific principle of aesthetics and to defend it against all other merely logical methods as the real source of all sound knowledge."[10]

Cassirer's narrative makes a nice story—an account of the linear progression from Cartesian rationalism to introspective empiricism, from reason to imagination, from correctness to sensitivity. Cassirer omits the Sublime, however. Its paradoxical nature, its noncoherence with *L'Art poétique,* does not fit into his story. Boileau's French translation of the pseudo-Lon-

ginian *On the Sublime* appeared in 1674, the same year as
L'Art poétique.[11] Accompanied by a preface that endeavored to
separate the Sublime in art from the sublime or high style,
Boileau's translation and his interpretation of the Sublime celebrated inarticulate, sudden emotive response in discourse and
in art. Boileau's insistence on simplicity of expression, grandeur of conception, and immediacy of aesthetic response placed
his theory of the Sublime in uneasy juxtaposition with the
strictures of *L'Art poétique*.

During his exchanges with Perrault, Fontenelle, and other
moderns, Boileau was challenged to define this concept which
he had posed as a touchstone of neoclassical criticism.[12] He
never produced a precise definition, although he did provide examples—the *fiat lux* passage of Genesis, passages from Cor-
neille's *Horace* and *Medée*.[13] Did Boileau believe that defining
the concept of the Sublime would undermine his own insistence
that the experience of the Sublime was inchoate, ineffable, and
thus not precisely definable? Was his reliance upon examples a
form of resistance to the inexorable rationalism of the moderns? It is likely that it was, for Boileau, an early Cartesian
himself, was known in his later life to have said that Descartes'
philosophy had ruined poetry through the indiscriminate application of mathematical principles.[14] Boileau probably intended the Sublime as his own antidote to neoclassical rigidity,
but his motives need not detain us here. What is significant for
understanding the impact of the Bolevian Sublime is to recognize how Boileau himself altered the pseudo-Longinian original
and to consider what became of this altered Sublime in eighteenth-century belletrism. The present chapter thus has two
purposes: first, to examine carefully Boileau's manipulations of
the Greek text so as to clarify his critical agenda, and second,
to consider subsequent treatments of the Sublime in the rhetorics of Joseph Priestley, George Campbell, and Hugh Blair. To
understand the significance of Boileau's work, however, one
must begin by considering the nature and fortunes of his
French translation of the Greek text.

Boileau and the Sublime

When Boileau first published his translation as part of his
Oeuvres diverses, he had a particular end in mind. Writing in

an era in which literacy had become widespread and in which the reading public was a heterogenous lot, Boileau was concerned about the standards of literary aesthetics. Hack playwrights and novelists had produced a variety of aberrations — the *burlesque,* preciosity, the mixture of genres — that Boileau had condemned and sought to suppress.[15] Hence, Boileau posed the Sublime as a critical standard for judging the merit of eloquence and literature. In the preface to his 1674 edition, Boileau described the Sublime as "the extraordinary and marvelous which is affecting in discourse and which causes a work to charm, delight, and transport [the listener or reader]."[16/a] Originating in creative genius and marked by simple expression and great thoughts, the true Sublime had an inevitable effect upon its audience. It "raises the soul, and brings it to conceive a high opinion of itself, filling it with joy and a sort of noble pride. . . ."[17/b] In commenting on the importance of effect in conceptions of the Sublime, Jules Brody has noted that "passion as an ingredient of sublimity is not the mere expression of a subjective state of mind, but an instrument of literary effect whose use, dictated by 'the nature of the subject' and the timeliness of the moment, is geared to a definite end."[18] And Julian Eugene White has said that as a defining criterion of the Sublime, "the emotion evoked in the audience is of paramount importance. The author's own feeling is of little value unless he is able to evoke in his readers a corresponding emotion."[19]

Because of preoccupation with audience response, the Sublime was the most rhetorical of literary concepts. Boileau's use of this concept to capture the imagination of his Western European contemporaries and of critics and theorists of the eighteenth century could hardly have been more successful. The scope and extent of Bolevian influence was described succinctly by the Loeb translator of the Greek text: "the records of 'antiquity' contain no reference to this treatise, and its existence was unknown until Robortello published it at Basle in 1554. . . .

---

a. cet extraordinaire et ce merveilleux qui frape dans le discours, et qui fait qu'un ouvrage enleve, ravit, transporte.

b. élève l'âme, et luy fait concevoir une plus haute opinion d'elle-mesme, la remplissant de joye et de je ne sçai quel noble orgueil. . . .

During the following hundred years [it] remained a close preserve for scholars until in 1674 Boileau published his translation, which was re-issued more than twenty times in the next
hundred years. From that moment, 'Longinus on the Sublime'
won fame commensurate with his merits."[20] In France, many
readers who had been denied access to the Greek text came to
see the French version very much as a new original.[21] Fénelon,
an excellent Hellenist himself, lifted verbatim passages from
Boileau's translation in his *Lettre à l'Académie*.[22] Lamy and
Rollin also cited and discussed Boileau's Sublime when they
considered the effects of style upon audiences.[23]

In Britain, the concept of the Sublime came to be invested
with considerable theoretical significance. Discussed at length
by John Holmes (1739), Edmund Burke (1757), John Lawson
(1758), Lord Kames (1762), Adam Smith (ca. 1763), and others,
the Sublime clearly became a standard *topos* of eighteenth-century critical theory.[24] To a considerable extent, critical preoccupation with the concept must be credited to Boileau. Before
his translation, allusions to *On the Sublime* were limited to
scholastics who could read Greek or one of the extant Latin
translations, and the treatise was viewed as a rhetorical *techne*
of interest to only a fraction of the reading public.[25] After the
translation, nearly every British theorist attended to the concept, either to draw attention to the Bolevian view or explicitly
to reject it.

In eighteenth-century Britain, the topic of the Sublime provided an excellent cross section of existing theoretical orientations. Once under way, interest in the Sublime assumed various
forms as various theorists differed on its nature, function, importance, and stylistic features. While some privileged the Sublime, viewing it as marvelous and rare, others sought to
dismantle and analyze the concept. While some emphasized
the intellective dimension of the sublime response, others insisted upon the pathetic. Subsequent theorists' conceptions of
the Sublime were tied to their views on the relations between
cognition and emotions in persuasion. In any case, the fortunes
of the Sublime in the eighteenth century began with the alterations and manipulations of the concept effected by Boileau in
his translation and accompanying commentary.

Boileau as Strategic Translator

Had Boileau's rendition of *On the Sublime* closely followed the original, we would have to attribute influence to the treatise itself rather than to Boileau. Theories of translation in Boileau's day, however, gave considerable latitude to the translator who was expected to adapt and adjust the text to the contemporary taste of his readership.[26] And, as Clark has noted, "Boileau's translation is an extremely loose version of the Greek original."[27] Brody has systematically studied the alterations Boileau made as he translated and has established the fact that Boileau had a particular agenda in mind.[28] In order to establish the Sublime as a touchstone, he had to invest the concept with a rare and exceptional capacity to influence the reader or hearer of a text.

In his preface to the original translation, Boileau openly stated his intention to provide his readers with a translation adapted to the seventeenth-century critical milieu: "Let no one expect to find here a timid and scrupulous version of the words of Longinus. Although I have endeavored not to deviate in any spot from the rules of correct translation; I have allowed myself an honest liberty, especially in the passages referred to here. I thought that it was not simply a matter of translating Longinus here but of giving the public a treatise on the Sublime that could be useful.[29/c] The usefulness that Boileau envisioned led him to recast the Greek text as he translated. Whereas Longinus saw sublimity as originating in both conception and style, Boileau viewed the locus of the Sublime as the response of a hearer or reader of a text. Whereas Longinus set out to demystify sublimity by giving examples and showing how its effects were achieved, Boileau sought to envelop the Sublime in an aura of mystery and ineffability so that it was discernible only to a man of taste—the classical critic instantiated in Boileau himself. Longinus had identified five sources of sublimity—the

---

c. Qu'on ne s'attende pas pourtant de trouver ici une version timide et scrupuleuse des paroles de Longin. Bien que je me sois efforcé de ne me point écarter en pas un endroit des regles de la veritable traduction; je me suis pourtant donné une honneste liberté, sur tout dans les passages qu'il rapporte. J'ai songé qu'il ne s'agissoit pas simplement ici de traduire Longin; mais de donner au Public un Traité du Sublime, qui pût estre utile.

power of forming great conceptions, vehement and inspired passion, use of figures, noble diction, and dignified and elevated composition.[30] Through strategies of semantic enhancement and suppression throughout the translation, Boileau emphasized the first two and minimized the importance of the last three.

In skewing the Greek text to his own purposes, Boileau used a strategy of *dissociation*.[31] He set up a hierarchy in which "the Sublime," as durable, profound, and real, was to be valued over "the sublime style," deemed by Boileau to be ephemeral, deceptive, and only apparent. Boileau proposed that the traditional notion of the sublime style (figures of speech, complex syntax, elevated language) be separated from the Sublime (great conceptions simply expressed). He makes his strategy quite apparent in his preface to the work:

> It is necessary to know that by the Sublime, Longinus does not mean what orators call the sublime style but the extraordinary and marvelous which is moving in discourse and which causes a work to charm, delight, and transport [the reader]. The sublime style always calls for grand words; but the Sublime can be found in a single thought, in a single figure, in a single turn of phrase. . . . It is thus necessary to understand by the Sublime in Longinus the Extraordinary, the Surprising, and as I have translated it, the Marvelous in discourse.[32/d]

Boileau here employed three dissociative strategies to prepare readers for the Longinian text as he had recast it. First, he took advantage of the absence of a definition in the Greek text to provide his own definition—"the Extraordinary, the Surprising and the Marvelous in discourse." He thereby implied that the Sublime was manifest in particular passages having these effects rather than in a stylistic quality of discourse in general.

---

d. Il faut donc sçavoir que par Sublime, Longin n'entend pas ce que les Orateurs appellent le stile sublime: mais cet extraordinaire et ce merveilleux qui frape dans le discours, et qui fait qu'un ouvrage enleve, ravit, transporte. Le stile sublime veut toujours de grands mots; mais le Sublime se peut trouver dans une seule pensée, dans une seule figure, dans un seul tour de paroles. . . . Il faut donc entendre par Sublime dans Longin, l'Extraordinaire, le Surprenant, et comme je l'ai traduit, le Merveilleux dans le discours.

Second, he reified his use of the term by providing it with a definite article and a capital letter to distinguish it from the common use of "sublime" to refer to a level of style. To emphasize the uniqueness and power of the Sublime, Boileau continued this practice throughout the French text of his translation. Third, he encouraged his readers to devalue conventional notions of sublime style by equating them with the mere use of *grands mots*. Elevated vocabulary had nothing mysterious or ineffable about it; it was an obvious and mechanical attribute of discourse that could be used and observed by any writer or critic. It therefore lacked intrinsic value.

To elevate his notion of the Sublime over against the sublime style, Boileau emphasized its power, its uniqueness, and its rarity. He stressed its impact as an effect that could strike, ravish, and transport the soul and do so infallibly and memorably. Note his insertions into the text when he described the Sublime's effects: "For it does not persuade but *it delights,* it transports, *and produces in us a certain admiration mixed with astonishment and surprise* which is *an entirely different thing* from pleasing only or persuading."[33/e] Unlike mere persuasion, the Sublime fills recipients with awe, astonishment, and surprise and its effects are involuntary, instantaneous, and irresistible. As Brody has observed, Boileau introduced the notion of instantaneous effect "entirely on his own" and made foremost the qualities of intensity, spontaneity, and enthrallment.[34] The absence in the Greek text of any support for "ravit," "admiration," "étonnement," and "surprise" supports Brody's observation.

Having singled out the concept of the Sublime as an aesthetic touchstone, Boileau then endeavored to mystify it, to clothe it with an aura of ineffability and the *je ne sais quoi*. He spoke of it as "une certaine force de discours" which had "something magnificent of which the elegant and majestic obscurity causes us to imagine many things beyond what they seem to say."[35/f] In his translation, Boileau repeatedly connected allu-

---

e. Car il ne persuade pas proprement, mais il *ravit,* il transporte, *et produit en nous une certaine admiration mêlée d'étonnement et de surprise,* qui est *toute autre chose* que de plaire seulement, ou de persuader.

f. quelque chose de magnifique, et dont l'obscurité elegante et majestueuse nous fait concevoir beaucoup de choses au delà de ce qu'elles semblent dire.

sions to the Sublime with gratuitous expressions such as *une certaine* and *je ne sais quoi* to suggest intuitive, irrational, indefinable elements.[36] His attempts at mystification enhanced the reader's conception of the Sublime as a valued term. Unlike the sublime style, marked by stylistic embellishments readily recognizable to all, the Sublime was ineffable and made manifest only in certain conditions.

The Essence of the Sublime: Boileau's Subsequent Commentary

Given the ineffability of the Sublime, its occurrence and specific qualities were not apparent to many readers of the Bolevian translation. Since the Sublime could be expressed in the simplest language, its external features clearly were not what distinguished it. Boileau's coyness about explicitly describing the concept eventually involved him in polemics with other critical theorists, and he was led to define and explain the concept further in critical reflections appended to the translation and included in a later edition of his *Oeuvres complètes*.

To be sublime, in Boileau's view, a passage had to be both natural and appropriate. The Sublime resulted when art and nature were so unified that art was hidden, invisible. The concept of the Sublime was thus tied to the then widely popular notions about naturalness and propriety.

As I noted earlier, the neoclassical conception of the natural was related, not to flora and fauna, but to a general conception of what was suitable and fitting.[37] Tied as it was to notions of *vraisemblance* and propriety, this idea of nature might seem abstract and ambiguous, but it assumed objectivity and status for neoclassical theorists and later for the British who found the concept attractive. For Boileau, a significant attribute of the Sublime was its capacity to strike just the right note, to unify all the elements of human nature so that the same thought expressed any other way would seem awkward or strained. Thus, the Sublime was artless, and Boileau could not resist strengthening further Longinus' already adamant suppression of the role of Art: "Art is *never in a higher state of perfection* than when it resembles Nature so strongly that one takes it for Nature itself; and on the contrary Nature never succeeds better than when art is hidden."[38/g]

In his Tenth Reflection, Boileau emphasized appropriateness by explaining that the Sublime resulted from a union of great thoughts, noble feelings, striking circumstances, and forceful expression. Boileau's flagship example of the Sublime was drawn from the *fiat lux* passage of Genesis: "God said, let there be light and there was light." To emphasize that style was not the essential ingredient, Boileau transposed the passage to the sublime style: "The sovereign Arbiter of nature in a single word formed the light," and he concluded that the passage as originally expressed "marks so well the obedience of the Creature to the Creator . . . and has something about it that is divine."[39/h] The Sublime, then, resulted from saying just what should be said in a given circumstance and no more. It expressed grandeur simply and responded nobly to the situation that gave rise to it. Boileau concluded that "In order to judge well the beautiful, the sublime, and the marvelous in the discourse, one should not simply consider what is said but the person who says it, the manner of speaking, and the occasion where it is said: so that it is necessary to consider, *non quid sit, sed quo loco sit.*"[40/i] Here we see rhetorical adaptation offered as an important factor in creating or destroying sublimity. Although logical processes of rhetorical invention were no longer given place, psychological and aesthetic adaptation were put forward as crucial to ideal communication. Invention was not described as a totally private act but as one combining individual judgment and perception with situational adaptations. In effect, a new canon of rhetoric was constructed.

In describing the qualities and effects of the Sublime, Boileau accomplished his dissociative task and identified a new

---

g. . . . l'Art *n'est jamais dans un plus haut degré de perfection,* que lorsqu'il ressemble si fort à la Nature, qu'on le prend pour la Nature même; et au contraire la Nature ne reüssit jamais mieux que quand l'Art est caché."

h. marque si bien l'obeissance de la Creature aux ordres du Createur . . . et a quelque chose de divin.

i. pour bien juger du Beau, du Sublime, du Merveilleux dans le Discours, il ne faut pas simplement regarder la chose qu'on dit, mais la personne qui la dit, la maniere dont on la dit, et l'occasion où on la dit: enfin qu'il faut regarder, *non quid sit, sed quo loco sit.*

aesthetic touchstone for classical criticism. By elevating two of the five Longinian sources of sublimity—grandeur of conception and vehement emotive response—Boileau suppressed the importance and role of style per se. He thus associated the Sublime with the natural and the substantial and the sublime style with the artificial and the formal. By introducing the terms "admiration," "delight," "astonishment," and "surprise" into his description of sublime response, Boileau emphasized the importance of instantaneous emotive response to a text. The conception of the Sublime thus contributed to the substitution of aesthetic for rational effects. As White observed, "the seventeenth century is the period *par excellence* of accommodation between reason and the art of pleasing."[41] Boileau's work was generative of the trend toward merging aesthetics and rationality.

The second book of John Holmes' *The Art of Rhetoric Made Easy,* which appeared at London in 1739, consisted entirely of a shortened version of *On the Sublime* with notes and commentary showing some Bolevian influence.[42] As the century progressed, however, British rhetoricians came under the influence of Joseph Addison and Francis Hutcheson, and direct Bolevian influence became harder to trace.[43] Nevertheless, Boileau brought the Sublime to the attention of critical theorists in France and Britain, made a distinction that took hold and became thematized in later work, and, as will be seen, introduced a notion later developed by Priestley, Campbell, and Blair.

Joseph Priestley's *Course of Lectures on Oratory and Criticism*

Sublimity became an important topic for British rhetoricians. Even Joseph Priestley, who avowedly sought to place his rhetorical theory on a scientific footing, felt the need to deal with this topic. Best known for his experiments with oxygen and his contributions to experimental science in the eighteenth century, Priestley also published his academic lectures on oratory and criticism, which were first delivered in 1762.[44] His motive in bringing them to press was to provide an illustration of David Hartley's doctrine of the association of ideas.[45] Bevilacqua and Murphy, editors of Priestley's lectures, have noted

Priestley's strategy in espousing Hartleian associationist psychology; he "employed the universal mode of inquiry to reduce seemingly irreducible phenomena of the mind to their simpler elements in much the same way as he reduced common air to simpler gasses. In both cases, Priestley sought to render given phenomena to as few causes as account entirely for observed effects."[46] Priestley's account of how the mind works and how discourse works upon the mind was avowedly reductionist. For him the cause of aesthetic response to discourse lay in the material objects it described and the associations made among them.

Priestley combined Hartleian psychology with the faculty psychology familiar in the eighteenth century. The different faculties (e.g., passions, judgment, imagination) are affected somewhat differently, but the basic process operates similarly. External objects are impressed on the senses and cause vibrations that convey sensations to the brain. These sensations only remain in the mind for a brief time, but, when repeated, leave vestiges or images of themselves that are the simple ideas of sensation from which complex ideas are made. Associations can now take place; ideas are connected by contiguity, resemblance, correspondence, and other means so that a given idea can trigger other associated ideas in various configurations.

Given this view of how the mind operates, one would expect Priestley's discussion of the Sublime to be based on mechanistic and materialistic principles. Unlike Boileau who emphasized the audience's emotive response as the determinative criterion for the Sublime, Priestley looked to sublimity in the objects conceived. In his view, the mind's contemplation of large or grand objects inspired contemplation of its own greatness, dignity, or importance. The response envisioned was more intellective than emotive: "the mind . . . conforming and adapting itself to the objects to which its attention is engaged must . . . enlarge itself, to conceive a great object."[47] When contemplating a grand or sublime object, the mind brings the imagination to bear to appreciate the strength and nature of its own powers. Priestley encouraged the rhetor to achieve such an effect in the most parsimonious manner possible. One should introduce as many sensible images as possible, avoid general abstract ideas and emphasize particulars, and use as few words as are neces-

sary to obtain an effect, thereby increasing the presence of
ideas associated with the one in question.[48]

Priestley made it clear that sublimity was effectuated
through comparison with other, lesser ideas. In particular, a
well-conducted climax was favorable to the Sublime because
each subsequent idea would be compared with the one before it
so as to make the final idea appear exceedingly large. Through
association, grandeur of conception could also result when we
connect the sublime object to its causes or to attributes usually
associated with it. For example, we could come to the sublime
conception of a palace by comparing it with other dwellings or
by considering the time and number of persons needed to erect
it.[49] These intermediate ideas are vehicular; they transport us
to the Sublime by means of comparison and association.

Also, objects, sentiments, and passions "of the first rank"
inspire sublimity. Natural objects, such as large rivers, high
mountains, extensive plains, the ocean, the heavens, thunder,
lightening, and earthquakes frequently engender the Sublime.
Likewise, human actions that produce great effects such as for-
titude, magnanimity, generosity, patriotism, and universal be-
nevolence can strike the mind with the idea of the Sublime.[50]
Abstract ideas, however, only derive their strength from association with their particular causes, adjuncts, or effects—
wealth with a large estate, power with the multitudes subject
to its control, honor with the achievements by which it was pro-
cured.[51]

In relation to the sublime style, Priestley did not make the
same distinctions or associations as Boileau. He did feel that
plain terms and simple expressions were most favorable to the
Sublime because they would keep attention focused on the sublimity of the object itself, but it was more essential to avoid
terms associated with trivial or mean objects. These would trigger secondary associations connected with such objects and
lower the conception itself. The associations connected with
words used were key and qualities of style were only of secondary importance. Neither did Priestley make a distinction between the Sublime and the sublime style in terms such as those
Boileau had used. He did, however, deprecate the bombastic or
hyperbolic style which was often used by writers who aimed at
the Sublime because "it is extremely easy in itself."[52]

In Priestley we see a conception of the Sublime that was in sharp contrast to Boileau's, yet the topic was sufficiently commonplace that he had to deal with it. As we might expect of a scientist, Priestley's main concern was to explain sublimity in objective, scientific terms. Whereas Boileau sought to mystify the phenomenon and invest it with the capacity to serve as an aesthetic, but nonetheless real, standard, Priestley considered sublimity one feature of discourse among others (e.g., novelty, beauty, uniformity, variety), and he sought to explain systematically how its effects were achieved and could be recognized. He did not view sublime response as primarily emotive or privileged, as Boileau did. Rather, for Priestley the Sublime resulted from an operation of intellect making use of imagination in associating an idea with other ideas. Achieving the Sublime derived from certain kinds of intellectual and imaginative processes governed by laws of the mind. Priestley thus employed Hartley's mixture of speculative physiology and psychology to dismantle the Sublime and to explain its workings by reference to what he took to be immutable patterns of human thought and perception. Unlike the materialist and determinative perspective offered by Priestley, George Campbell's rhetoric emphasized the Sublime's aesthetic qualities and employed them to set out his theory of genres.

George Campbell's *Philosophy of Rhetoric*

To appreciate George Campbell's treatment of the Sublime in his 1776 treatise on rhetoric, one should keep his purpose in mind. He set out, not to describe speaking practices, nor to offer practical rhetorical advice, nor to operate as a critic but, rather, to "canvass those principles in our nature to which the various attempts are adapted, and by which . . . their success or want of success may be accounted for."[53] In his effort to discover principles of human nature through the study of rhetoric, Campbell began by attempting to differentiate genres of discourse and to consider various reactions to them. He employed the Sublime as a means to assist him in this end, and hence its role in his *Philosophy* was somewhat subsidiary.

Campbell broadened the conception of eloquence and defined it as "that art or talent by which discourse is adapted to its end."[54] The ends of speaking were four in number—to enlighten understanding, please the imagination, move the passions, and influence the will. The Sublime played a significant role in fulfilling the second function—pleasing the imagination. Appeals to the imagination were significant because any one of the four functions might predominate in a discourse while the others played subservient roles as means.[55] Since the imagination could assist in moving the passions or the will, the Sublime could be important in those processes, too.

Like Fénelon, Campbell likened discursive communication to portraiture. Like the painter, the orator's task in part is imitation. Therefore, successful narration and description consist in constructing lively and beautiful representations. Campbell believed that two qualities were requisite to the Sublime in portrayals—dignity in the subject and manner of imitation, and resemblance.[56] To capture imagination, portrayals must be ingenious; those that compare highly similar or identical objects will not capture listeners' attention. But if subtle and uncommon resemblances are displayed in analogies, antitheses, and metaphors, and if such comparisons are brilliant and arresting, then the effect will be sublime. These comparisons must not be obtrusive or obvious in their artfulness, however, for Campbell would agree with Fénelon that "the beautiful which is only beautiful, that is, brilliant, is only half beautiful."[57/j]

Campbell's purpose in discussing the Sublime was different from Boileau's or Longinus'. He did not seek to invest the Sublime with special qualities or to mark it as an aesthetic touchstone. By connecting the Sublime to depiction, imitation, and pleasurable response, Campbell carved out a domain particular to the imagination and separate from the passions. The Sublime evoked admiration, not anger, ambition, or hope. What of the belief among Campbell's contemporaries that admiration itself is a passion?[58] Campbell responded by dissociating admiration from the passions: "Admiration . . . doth not require to its production, as the passions generally do, any reflex view of motives or tendencies, or of any relation either to private interest, or to the good of others; and ought therefore to be numbered among those original feelings of the mind . . . being of the

---

j. le beau qui n'est que beau, c'est à dire, brillant, n'est beau qu'à demi.

same class with a taste for beauty, an ear for music, or our moral sentiments."[59] Admiration was a reflex sense and was not connected to motives or private interest as were the passions. The sublime response consisted in admiration, which resulted from the intellective pleasure caused by recognizing a fine imitation, a painting of nature.

As perspicuity was the dominant quality of instructive discourse and vehemence of persuasion, so sublimity was conceived to be the dominant quality of discourse addressed to the imagination. Sublimity was not vehemence; the latter came from energetic expression, climactic arrangement, and exclamation. Many speeches are vehement but not sublime, and Campbell criticized Longinus for combining the two and for failing to distinguish among the faculties and among the senses of sublime as a critical concept: "Longinus' acceptation of the term *sublime* is extremely indefinite, importing an eminent degree of almost any excellence of speech, of whatever kind."[60] Unlike Longinus, Campbell sought a well demarcated conception and use for the term "sublime."

The extent of Bolevian influence on Campbell's conception of the Sublime is difficult to determine. Campbell read French, and in his *Philosophy of Rhetoric* he cited more than fifteen French authors, including Bouhours, Buffier, Dubos, Rollin, and Boileau.[61] But Campbell also read Greek, and so he may have read the pseudo-Longinian treatise in the original.[62] In any case, the use Campbell made of sublimity seems unique among his peers. The Sublime assisted Campbell in constructing a taxonomy of discursive genres. It served as a paradigm for one sort of discourse—that addressed to the imagination. It was particularly suited to imitation such as is found in narration, description, epic poetry, and certain modes of oratory. The Sublime was, in sum, excellence in portraiture; in display of great and noble images; and in uncommon and striking resemblances.

Hugh Blair's *Lectures on Rhetoric and Belles Lettres*

Priestley's and Campbell's discussions of the Sublime reflected a concern for its psychological elements and their importance. Priestley's dependence on Hartleian psychology and Campbell's on Humean empiricism caused their theories of the Sublime to be more scientific and less focused on emotive response than Boileau's. Such was not the case with Hugh Blair. His lectures, first published in 1783, were a compendium of rhetorical principles and exemplars originally intended for students who had had no preparatory study in rhetoric.[63] As Patricia Bizzell and Bruce Herzberg have observed, Blair's lectures fed "the popular desire for rules of taste, guidelines for writing and speaking, and well-digested, if not predigested, samples of popular literature."[64] Priestley and Campbell intended to break new ground, to provide scientific or philosophically grounded accounts of rhetoric. Blair's treatment, however, tended to be conservative and relatively traditional. Since Blair planned his *Lectures* as introductory, criticizing them for their lack of depth, penetration, and sophistication may be unfair.[65] In any case, Blair did not try to break new ground. He had neither the scientific aspirations of Priestley nor the scientific and philosophical interests of Campbell. He was content to reassert conventional, eighteenth-century ideas about rhetoric in clear and attractive fashion. In the last, he succeeded well, as the popularity of his *Lectures* attested.

Blair's *Lectures on Rhetoric and Belles Lettres* were eventually translated into five foreign languages and issued in sixty editions.[66] A melange of conventional wisdom, neoclassical and romantic doctrines, and contemporary and classical literary examples, they appealed to a wide range of audiences and quickly outpaced the works of Priestley, John Lawson, and other rhetoricians in readership.[67] Before and during their attendance at Blair's lectures, students at Edinburgh had been exposed to a broad curriculum including mathematics, natural philosophy, moral philosophy, logic, the history of philosophy, and modern languages as well as the classics.[68] Blair's purpose was thus to initiate his students into the study of belles lettres so as "to cultivate their Taste, to form their Style, or to prepare [them] for Public Speaking or Composition."[69] To do this, Blair said he would make use of whatever was useful and avail himself "of the ideas and reflections of others, as far as he thought them proper to be adopted."[70]

Blair's *Lectures* drew on a wide range of borrowings from

other authors, many of them unattributed. He made extensive use of Quintilian and Cicero on rhetorical theory, but he was also attracted to French critics and theorists. There are citations of over forty French authors in the two volumes of Blair's *Lectures;* Fénelon, Dubos, and Bernard le Bovier de Fontenelle receive multiple citations.[71] Blair's familiarity with and appreciation of French theorists and models might lead one to suspect that he arrived at his conception of sublimity by way of Boileau even if direct evidence were lacking.

In fact, Blair's view of the Sublime is Bolevian on every major issue Blair raised. Blair did not hesitate to invest the Sublime with the unique and ineffable properties attributed to it by Boileau: "It consists in a kind of admiration and expansion of the mind; it raises the mind above its ordinary state; and fills it with a degree of wonder and astonishment, which it cannot well express."[72] Blair thereby located the Sublime in the emotional response of the hearer or reader, and he pressed this theme throughout his subsequent discussion. Having provided a number of examples of sublimity in objects and descriptions, he concluded by observing that "in all these instances, the emotion raised in us is of the same kind, although the objects that produce them be of widely different kinds."[73] Not only did Blair emphasize emotive response, he included in the Sublime two attributes inserted by Boileau—attributes that did not occur in the Greek treatise—admiration and astonishment.

In Blair's fourth lecture, he summarized the five sources of sublimity listed in *On the Sublime*—boldness and grandeur in thoughts, the pathetic, the proper application of figures, the use of tropes and beautiful expressions, and musical structure and arrangement of words.[74] Like Boileau, Blair felt that only the first two were characteristic of the truly Sublime, and he even criticized Longinus for confusing the concept! "He sets out, indeed, with describing [the Sublime] in its just and proper meaning; as something that elevates the mind above itself, and fills it with high conceptions, and a noble pride. But from this view of it he frequently departs; and substitutes in the place of it, whatever, in any strain of composition, pleases highly."[75]

Blair then continued by explicitly citing Boileau on the distinction between the sublime style and the true Sublime: "As for what is called the Sublime Style, it is, for the most part, a very bad one; and has no relation whatever to the real Sublime."[76] Blair distinguished the sublimity of the *fiat lux* passage from the Bolevian paraphrase of it and concluded that, "as Boileau has well observed the style is indeed raised but the thought is fallen."[77] What, then, was the source of the Sublime? Blair was emphatic in his insistence that it did not arise from characteristics of the discourse itself: "It is not by hunting after tropes, and figures, and rhetorical assistances, that we can expect to produce it. No: it stands clear . . . of these laboured refinements of art. It must come unsought, if it come at all; and be the natural offspring of a strong imagination."[78]

A necessary feature of the Sublime for Blair as for Boileau was appropriateness. Blair emphasized the need to select circumstances that best displayed the object of conception. Circumstances appropriately selected "exhibit the object in its full and most striking point of view."[79] If the circumstances were too general, the object would only be portrayed in a faint light. If they were mean or trivial, the whole would be degraded. The Sublime thus consisted of a strong and vivid conception whose most powerful and vivid features were strikingly portrayed.

Thus, on nearly every major point of his discussion, Blair perpetuated Boileau's view of the Sublime. He emphatically distinguished it from the high style and attempted to identify it with simple expression. He claimed that its effects were powerful, irresistible, and instantaneous and thus could not be sustained in long passages. He located the criterion of the Sublime in the response to it, in which the mind is elevated above its natural state and filled with enthusiasm, surprise, and awe. And Blair emphasized the role of appropriateness—that circumstances selected for portrayal should be artfully matched to the grandeur of the object or event portrayed. The only Bolevian characteristic absent from Blair's account was an effort to mystify the concept. Unlike Boileau, Blair seemed concerned to identify the Sublime's major features explicitly and to spell them out in his lectures. As will be seen in chapter 4, Blair's attempts at demystification extended to his account of taste which applied Humean empiricism and argued that taste grew from experience and education and thus could be acquired by his students and readers.

Conclusion

In translating *On the Sublime* and in commenting on its theory, Boileau sought to reify the Sublime and invest it with unique properties so that it could function as a critical touchstone. He identified a particular kind of emotive response—admiration, surprise, awe, astonishment—as the defining characteristic of the Sublime, and he ascribed an exceptional status to the Sublime as a rare and extraordinary phenomenon. Boileau's success in exploiting the Sublime is evinced by the frequency with which subsequent theorists cited him or responded to his position. Their varying interpretations indicate the concept's widespread functions and uses in the diverse strands of eighteenth-century rhetorical theory.

The use made of the Sublime in the rhetorical theories of Priestley, Campbell, and Blair shows the malleability of the concept. In Priestley's materialist conception, the Sublime was used to show the relationship between the natural world and mental conceptions of it. Objects that were sublime could create expansiveness and a feeling of grandeur in the mind as long as the rhetor avoided reference to trivial or mean objects. In Campbell's philosophical examination of discourse and human nature, the concept of the Sublime was used to identify a particular genre of discourse—that addressing the imagination. In this theory, sublime responses could be evoked through vivid and striking portraitures and use of uncommon resemblances. Of the three theories, Blair's came closest to Boileau's and in fact was extensively dependent on it. Like Boileau, Blair believed that the defining characteristic of the Sublime was its capacity to rouse the passions of an audience. By arguing persistently that the Sublime could be identified only by its effect upon a listener and its evocation of grandeur and awe, Blair perpetuated the Bolevian view and ensured its continued dissemination into the nineteenth century.

In each of the three British theories, too, the Sublime illustrated the rapprochement between cognition and emotion in eighteenth-century rhetorics. For Priestley, the sublime response was elicited by sublime objects, sentiments, and passions. The rhetor's essential task was to create conceptions of the Sublime by focusing attention on objects of great magnitude and grandeur. For Campbell, the imagination could be excited by the juxtaposition of unique resemblances and associations in vivid portraiture. For Blair, grand conceptions and noble sentiments simply expressed could be called sublime if they raised the mind above its ordinary state and filled it with awe and wonder. As in Boileau, in Blair's conception the Sublime could be identified only in virtue of the response engendered in a reader or hearer. In these three theories the sublime response, while immediate and involuntary, assumed cognitive elements through principles of association and division among the faculties.

All of these authors perceived in the Sublime an opportunity to identify discursive features that excited a strong, memorable response from an audience. For them, the Sublime was paradigmatic; it aroused admiration and awe and excited the imagination. Describing its workings enabled Priestley and Campbell to explain how discourse worked upon the mind; their accounts of the psychological impact of rhetoric were thus furthered by the Sublime. For Boileau and for Blair, the Sublime served as a critical touchstone and a criterion by which the quality of discourse could be judged. In all cases, because of its fusion of aesthetics and *pathos,* the Sublime provided an essential dimension of the sixth canon.

Chapter 4

Taste

French conceptions of taste at the turn of the eighteenth century were varied. Fénelon's taste standard was embodied in "the natural," derived from a "nature" that was symmetrical and refined. For Boileau, taste was instantiated in the critic of discernment who could instinctively recognize the Sublime because of innate aesthetic sensibility. Rollin emphasized the importance of familiarity with *belles lettres* and education as means of acquiring taste. These theorists' positions dramatize many issues concerning taste that occupied both French and Scottish critics: Was there a universal standard of taste or was taste relative? Was taste innate or was it acquired? If acquired, what method of improvement was best—study of aesthetic principles or of the great models of art and literature? In both France and Scotland during the Enlightenment, taste was an ever-present and significant concern.

It was of vital interest because reading, attending plays and performances, and discussing the literary merit of various works provided the primary form of leisure entertainment in both French and Scottish culture. As Rémy Saisselin has said of this period, "Taste . . . was inseparable from worldly skepticism, civility, and the flowering of a polite society. . . . Taste was what made life tolerable. It determined the *décor* within which one lived; it allowed one to live with oneself as well as with others; it was the manner of judging the arts as well as the sciences. . . . Taste was an over-all principle whereby one attempted the creation of a civilized human order."[1] Rollin said of taste, "In a word, the quality most necessary . . . for the entire conduct of life is this taste, this prudence, this discernment which teaches on each matter and each occasion what one should do and how one should do it."[2/a] Recognizing his stu-

---

a. En un mot, la qualité la plus nécessaire, non seulement pour l'art de parler et pour les sciences, mais pour toute la conduite de la vie, est ce goût, cette prudence, ce discernement, qui apprend en chaque matière et en chaque occasion, ce qu'il faut faire, et comment il faut le faire.

dents' desire to acquire such discernment, Hugh Blair assured them that familiarity with the arts would enable them to practice "true criticism." "True criticism is a liberal and humane art. It is the offspring of good sense and refined taste. It aims at acquiring a just discernment of the real merit of authors. . . . It teaches us, in a word, to admire and to blame with judgment, and not to follow the crowd blindly."[3] Taste was the means of demonstrating that one was fit for cultured life in a cultured society.

Study of taste was also a means to improve understanding of human nature. As Blair further observed, disquisitions on aesthetic principles "are very intimately connected with knowledge of ourselves. They necessarily lead us to reflect on the operations of the imagination, and the movements of the heart, and increase our acquaintance with some of the most refined feelings which belong to our frame."[4] Eighteenth-century aestheticians sought to establish rational and scientific grounds for taste. They distinguished varieties of aesthetic experience, isolated the causes of psychological response, and discussed the mechanisms of causation.[5] In so doing, they hoped to explain how the mind worked.

As I have shown, the rhetorics of this period were situated in a belletristic system that coupled eloquence with literature. Since discourse was deemed most effective when it worked like portraiture, Blair and Campbell dwelt extensively on aesthetic topics.[6] For example, Campbell included among his genres discourse intended to please the imagination. Furthermore, he observed that imagistic appeals should figure in all kinds of speaking, since lively depiction and vivid imagery were the primary and inevitable means of moving the passions and thus influencing the will.[7] In any system so fundamentally tied to the imagination and to sensory stimulation, taste would play an important role.

Emphasis on taste meant that rhetoric's historical preoccupation with production and with the speaker's purpose was supplanted by a nearly exclusive emphasis upon reception. It is one thing to ask how speakers can draw upon audiences' beliefs to construct arguments, or how they can couch self-descriptions and introductions so as to appear in the best possible light. It was quite another to focus on the psychological processes brought into play when audiences heard and responded to discourse. Why were certain narratives and descriptions affecting while others missed the mark? How were various emotions ordered and related to one another? Why did some people appreciate and enjoy a work while others disliked it? Was there any consensus concerning the artistic merit of various discursive forms? Answers to such questions provided the intellectual frameworks upon which most eighteenth-century rhetorics were constructed.

Blair's and Campbell's positions on such matters can be understood only in terms of the intellectual milieu in which they worked. Eighteenth-century Scottish theorists of taste were more or less divided into two camps—the empiricists led by David Hume and the commonsense philosophers who followed Thomas Reid. As I will establish later, Blair and Campbell folded both empiricism and commonsense philosophy into their theories of taste. Both of them had read and heard Hume and Reid and both knew them personally, and each of the two rhetoricians selectively included the ideas of both men in his theory of taste.[8] Their combinations of empiricist and commonsense aesthetics will be better understood if the tenets of each of the two orientations are first made explicit.

An Empiricist View of Taste: Hume and Gerard

In eighteenth-century theories of taste, certain issues relating to the nature and faculty of taste became standard *topoi*. These included whether the beautiful arose from sensory response or from the qualities of the object itself, whether taste was innate or acquired, and whether the standard of taste was vested in the general public or in some intellectual elite. Empiricists such as Hume and Alexander Gerard looked to sensory response to resolve such questions, whereas commonsense philosophers emphasized innate sensibility, judgment, and application of aesthetic principles. Since the commonsense philosophers wrote in response to the Humeans, my account will begin with essays on taste by Hume and Gerard.

David Hume's "Of the Standard of Taste" first appeared in 1757 and was considered by Hume to be his primary contribution to criticism.[9] Gerard's *An Essay on Taste* was written soon after and submitted for a competition sponsored by the Select Society of Edinburgh. It was awarded the premium as the best essay on taste and was published in 1759.[10] Although Gerard belonged to the philosophical society in Aberdeen founded by Reid and although he was influenced by commonsense principles, the bulk of Gerard's theory of taste derived from Hume. Walter Hipple has observed that "the *Essay on Taste* is an essay in faculty psychology. And the writer to whom Gerard owes most is Hume. Like Hume, he is a reductionist."[11] Hipple has further observed that those commonsense principles that did influence Gerard had much greater impact in his theology and cosmology than in his aesthetics. Close examination of Gerard's principles of taste consistently reveals a pervasive Humean influence. Indeed, whereas Hume limited his explicit statements on taste to a brief essay, Gerard produced an extensive discussion carrying the Humean perspective to many issues that Hume neglected or treated only briefly.[12]

Hume's perspective on aesthetic response can be understood if one begins with an observation about his philosophy by D. G. C. MacNabb: "[Hume] was unable entirely to throw off a picture of the mind that, with slight variations, had dominated philosophical thinking for over a century. The mind was pictured as an immaterial thing with the powers of receiving representations of things in the world which it inhabits, of reasoning about these representations, and of making decisions that are somehow translated into physical action by the body to which the mind is temporarily attached. These representations were usually called 'ideas.' "[13] This picture of the mind denied the existence of innate ideas and instead represented the mind as progressively formed by sensory experience of the world around it. One would expect anyone holding this *tabula rasa* view of the mind to identify the sensory pleasure evoked by beauty as the locus of the beautiful, and that is indeed what Hume did.

When Hume discussed taste, he rejected rationalism as its source. "It is evident that none of the rules of composition are fixed by reasonings *a priori*. . . . their foundation is the same with that of all the practical sciences, *experience,* nor are they anything but general characteristics concerning *what has been*

universally found to please in all countries in all ages."[14] For
Hume, the standard of taste was thus located in the percipient's sensory response and sentiments, and it was developed
from experience. But this locus of taste was not in just any person but occurred in an idealized percipient. Hume disparaged
the capacity of "the generality of men" to form a standard; instead, he invested the requisite powers of discrimination in
what he called "a true judge."[15] In order to provide a critical
touchstone, however, this hypothetical person must possess
certain qualifications and characteristics. Most of Hume's essay
is devoted to describing the necessary attributes of this true
judge, and nearly all of them have to do with his sensory
makeup.

First, there being a strong resemblance between bodily and
mental taste, one must have good organs of perception. "In each
creature," Hume observed, "there is a sound and a defective
state; and the former alone can be supposed to afford us a true
standard of taste and sentiment."[16] Just as a man in a fever
would be unable to judge flavors, or one with jaundice to evalu-
ate colors, so is anyone with impaired perceptive organs unqualified to judge the beauty of an object. Likewise, the
conditions of perceiving should be propitious: the time and
place must be proper; the imagination suitably disposed; and
the mind serene and attentive.[17]

Second, a "true judge" would possess delicacy of taste. Delicacy is present whenever "the organs are so fine, as to allow
nothing to escape them; and at the same time so exact as to
perceive every ingredient in the composition."[18] To illustrate,
Hume recounted a story from *Don Quixote:*

> Two . . . kinsmen were once called to give their opinion of
> a hogshead, which was supposed to be excellent, being old
> and of a good vintage. One of them tastes it; considers it;
> and after mature reflection pronounces the wine to be
> good, were it not for a small taste of leather, which he
> perceived in it. The other, after using the same precau-
> tions, gives also his verdict in favour of the wine; but with
> the reserve of a taste of iron, which he could easily distin-
> guish. You cannot imagine how much they were both ridi-
> culed for their judgment. But who laughed in the end? On

> emptying the hogshead, there was found at the bottom,
> an old key with a leathern thong tied to it.[19]

In Hume's view, delicacy of taste yields subtle perceptions, con-firmed in this example by finding the key. Delicacy enables one to locate patterns that justify a given judgment—of wine or of compositions. Delicacy enables a "true judge" to perceive the most minute phenomena exactly, to detect blemishes that oth-ers fail to see, and to make further discriminations. Delicacy enables one to silence an inferior critic by showing where he has gone wrong. It provides the grounds of accurate judgment and intelligible explanation. Further, it is acquired by experi-ence.

Third, since taste is founded on experience, "nothing tends further to encrease and improve this talent, than *practice* in a particular art, and the frequent survey or contemplation of a particular species of beauty."[20] Critics can judge unfamiliar ob-jects only with difficulty, because their conceptions of them are often "obscure and confused." Familiarity with a genre of ob-jects, however, enables critics' sentiments to become clear and distinct and their feelings more exact. With practice, "the mist dissipates, which seemed to hang formerly over the object. The organ acquires greater perfection in its operations; and can pronounce, without danger of mistake, concerning the merits of every performance."[21]

Fourth, a "true judge" must have made comparisons be-tween several species and degrees of art. Hume believed that a person who had not compared different kinds of beauty was unqualified to pronounce an opinion with regard to aesthetic objects. Only exposure to many performances produced in dif-ferent ages and nations could enable the "true judge" to "rate the merits of a work exhibited to his view, and assign its proper rank among productions of genius."[22]

Fifth, the "true judge" should be free of prejudice. Hume observed that "every work of art, in order to produce its due effect on the mind, must be surveyed in a certain point of view, and cannot be relished by persons, whose situation, real or imaginary, is not conformable to that which is required by the performance."[23] Orators speak to audiences that have their own particular interests, opinions, passions, and prejudices, and orators are obliged in their role as persuaders to adapt to the audiences' predispositions. Critics judging such oratory should place themselves in the same situation as the audience in order to form a true judgment of any oration. Likewise, in judging anyone's work, the critic should set aside any personal friendship or enmity with the author and judge the work on its merits. A prejudiced critic is like a crooked ruler; he cannot measure a work's merits because of the perversion of his own sentiments. Here again we see Hume fine-tuning the instrument in which the standard of taste is to be found.

Finally, the "true judge" must possess "good sense." "Good sense" consists in the capacity to judge a work's propriety and coherence. Is the work consistent and coherent? Is it well adapted to its end or purpose? Is the reasoning just? Are its characters portrayed in a manner conforming with their personalities and circumstances? Here Hume seemed aware that he was moving away from his insistence that taste was to be developed through cumulative sensory experience and the sentiments of the percipient. Since good sense depends upon a cognitive judgment of a work, Hume hedged his position by observing that "reason, *if not an essential part of taste, is at least* requisite to the operations of this latter faculty [good sense]."[24]

Hume, then, located the standard of taste in a hypothetical ideal possessed of strong organs, delicacy, practice in judging objects of a given genre and in comparing various objects, and freedom from prejudice. Hume's position was not without problems. First, he rejected the taste of the generality of men and privileged the "true judge." Blessed by unusual delicacy, this individual could presumably detect excellence and defects unnoticed by others. But how was delicacy to be acquired? "[T]he best way of ascertaining it," Hume argued, "is to appeal to those models and principles which have been established by the uniform consent and experience of nations and ages."[25] Here one is referred to that general standard of taste that Hume elsewhere had rejected.

Second, there was the problem of where the "true judges" were to be found. How could they be differentiated from mere pretenders? Hume admitted that such questions "are embarrassing; and seem to throw us back into the same uncertainty, from which, during the course of this essay, we have endeavored to extricate ourselves."[26] Hume's recourse was to insist that such critics did exist, that their role was valuable and estimable, and that their existence was a matter of fact and not of sentiment. Such matters, Hume said, "will be agreed on by all mankind."[27] So, although there was no general agreement on the identity of these judges, everyone would agree that they existed, somewhere. Hume's position seems unsatisfying. General approbation and agreement seemed a sine qua non of his theory, however much he sought to deny it. And the sensate experience and sentiment of these judges was hardly an empirical criterion, since the judges themselves could not be precisely identified.

Gerard, who followed Hume in nearly all the other major features of his own aesthetic theory, took exception to Hume's recourse to "true judges" as sources of a standard of taste. Gerard seemed to recognize the implicit difficulties in Hume's position, particularly in regard to who these true judges were. Gerard accurately characterized Hume's position as follows:

> The sentiments of those only are to be taken into account, who have a good natural taste, who have not allowed it to be vitiated, who have improved it by study or conversation, and by such extensive acquaintance with works of imagination, as enables them to compare one with others and to judge of its relative as well as of its intrinsic merit: and the sentiments, even of persons thus qualified, are to be respected with respect to a particular work, only when they have come to the examination of it with serenity of mind, in a disposition fit for giving its several beauties and blemishes their due influence upon them; when they have examined it with attention; when they have studied it deliberately, and surveyed it in every different point of view.[28]

Gerard here effectively summarized Hume's position. He then put forward three serious objections to Hume's ascription of a taste standard to a group of idealized critics.

First, since this group of true judges belong to a particular culture and time, they are bound tacitly to adopt the implicit tastes and proclivities of that time. Hume's standard was there-

fore ethnocentric, in Gerard's view. The Western world may
have universally admired Homer's *Iliad,* Euripides' and Sopho-
cles' tragedies, and Demosthenes' orations. "But," Gerard
asked, "does this amount to the consent of all ages and nations?
Not at all."[29] While Europeans might approve such works because they are similar to their own sentiments and manners,
Asiatics would not. One culture might praise works for their
elegance, purity, and sedateness of reason, while another
might condemn the same works for a cold spirit and lack of
imagination. Such differences cannot be resolved solely
through recourse to a percipient standard of taste.

Second, such a standard relies overmuch on the circumstances of an artist's production. A rare genius might very pos-
sibly arise in an obscure, out-of-the-way setting and remain
unknown because he or she was not recognized by the right
people. As Gerard argued, "if the extent of the approbation
which a work obtains, depend [sic] so much on the celebrity of
the country where it is produced, and on other circumstances
wholly accidental or extraneous, it cannot alone or immediately
be the measure of its intrinsic merit."[30] In light of this objection, Hume's percipient standard was made to seem quite cir-
cumstantial in its application.

Finally, Gerard leveled his most damaging objection
against any standard of taste grounded in general approbation.
If the only source of experience for judging a work is past experience, what is to be done about striking originality? The
very value of truly original works is their departure from what
preceded them. Gerard noted that "the greater the originality
which they possess, the more unlike they will be to the works
which men have been accustomed to admire; habit will prevent
their relishing their beauties."[31]

Gerard believed that the only way out of these difficulties
was to appeal to general rules of criticism or general principles
of human nature. These rules were to be "derived from criticism and philosophy [and] not affected by . . . accidental advan-
tages and disadvantages."[32] Gerard believed that there were
principles common to everyone's experience that could be used
as a resource to establish a standard of taste. In fact, one of his
purposes in *An Essay on Taste* was to articulate such principles.

Hipple has noted that Gerard's position on a taste standard

was not added to his work (as its fourth part) until twenty-two years after the *Essay*'s original publication.[33] In the first three parts of the work, Gerard endeavored to explain systematically the origin, workings, and development of taste by means of Humean associationist principles. Gerard's detailed examination of this "mental chemistry" attempted to identify sources of pleasure in the human psyche when it encounters beautiful, novel, or sublime objects.

In regard to novelty, for example, Gerard explained that "the elevation and exertion of mind which springs from the mere difficulty of conceiving a new object, or from the liveliness of a new perception, is attended with surprise, which augments our delight or uneasiness, by farther enlivening the thought, and agitating the mind."[34] It is for this reason that orators avoid modes of expression that are trite and common. Only by ingenious use of figures, images, and illustrations can they attract attention and "surprise by the unexpectedness of their introduction."[35] Large objects expand the mind, filling it "with one grand sensation, which totally possessing it, composes it into a solemn sedateness, and strikes it with deep silent wonder and admiration. . . ."[36] Orators may achieve this effect by describing the sublime, either of nature or of passions and character, or they may render something grand by associating it with sublime objects through analogy.

The style of expression directly affects the mind's responses to discourse. Perspicuity enables the mind to conceive easily of an object and thus to think well of itself, whereas obscurity "occasions an uneasy search into the meaning of parts, or the tendency of the whole, which requires greater labor than we are willing to bestow."[37] Use of figures and images in vivid portraiture facilitates the sensory response of the audience. In fact, poetry and oratory being more imperfectly mimetic than painting, must rely on suggestion and thus have a special kind of merit.[38]

As Marjorie Grene has argued, Gerard's observations constitute a "reflex sense" theory of taste.[39] In this account, the mind experiences pleasure by conforming itself to objects. The mental action of conceiving the object is what causes pleasure. Gerard's reflex sense theory suggested such principles as:

—The manner of portraying an object affects how it is conceived.

—Sublime objects should be simply portrayed, or the mind will contemplate not one, but many small objects.

—Portrayals should be lively and ingenious so as to hold attention.

—The difficulty of the portrayal will heighten the mind's idea of the skill of execution.

Could these have been the "principles" to which Gerard alluded in his refutation of Hume? Of course, they were, and the ingeniousness of Gerard's thinking was that he was able to generalize the Humean orientation into principles that provided an infrastructure necessary but missing in Hume. Hume's insistence upon an idealized percipient as the locus of a taste standard left Hume in a cul-de-sac and forced him into circular theorizing. When Gerard successfully articulated associationist principles as the basis of aesthetic judgment, he discovered a means of generalizing a taste standard consistent with Hume's own position.

Because of the way Reid will responded to Hume (and to Gerard), we must explicitly consider the relation of sensate response and cognitive judgment in Gerard's theory of taste. Gerard wanted to establish a theory of taste based on associationist principles, and yet he had also to account for judgment. His position, simply put, was this: simple taste was an internal reflex sense derived from sensation; *good* taste, however, involved judgment.

Following Hume, Gerard believed that all the phenomena of taste "proceed, either from the general laws of *sensation,* or from certain operations of the *imagination.* . . . [Taste] supplies us with simple perceptions, entirely different from all that we receive by external sense, or by reflection. . . . [T]aste exhibits a set of perceptions which . . . result from, but are not included in, the primary and direct perception of objects. They are however equally uncompounded in their feeling, as incapable of being conceived prior to experience, as immediately, necessarily, and regularly exhibited in certain circumstances, as any other sensations whatsoever."[40] In a note appended to this passage, Gerard clarified for his reader the differences between an internal reflex sense such as taste and reasoning. A sense supplies simple perceptions; these are received immediately, prior to any reasoning concerning the qualities of the object or the causes of the sensation. Internal reflex sensory response is independent of volition; given the right circumstances, such sensations cannot be altered or prevented by any act of will.[41]

The processes of reasoning, on the other hand, are derived and compounded rather than immediate. "We do not prove, that certain objects are grand by arguments, but we perceive them to be grand in consequence of the natural constitution of our mind, which disposes us, without reflection, to be pleased with largeness and simplicity."[42] The deductions and operations of reason are complex and volitional, unlike exercise of taste, wherein the mind conforms itself immediately to the object. This is not to say that judgment has no role in taste, however. Earlier in the *Essay,* Gerard had observed that the reflex sense of taste and the cognitive processes of judgment generally operate together to form good taste. In the operations of taste, judgment presents subjects on which the senses exercise themselves, compares and weighs their perceptions, and evaluates the whole.[43] Taste enables one to feel what pleases or displeases, but judgment allows one to know what ought to gratify or disgust. In other words, sensation forms the sine qua non of taste, but it is rarely found to operate in the absence of judgment.

Gerard's belief that sensation and not cognition was the source of taste distinguished Gerard from Reid and the commonsense theorists. Gerard's theory of taste was profoundly empirical and associationist in its orientation, and the principles of judgment in taste admitted by Gerard were themselves based on empirical principles. A rhetorical theory based on Gerard's views would consider discourse as made up of elements experienced as beautiful, sublime, picturesque, ridiculous, ugly, and so forth. Judgment entered into the picture only when a reader or critic endeavored to understand or justify his sensation after the fact. For commonsense theorists like Reid, the equation was to be reversed. Cognition and an internal sense of beauty preceded aesthetic appreciation. And, as will be seen in the case of Reid, this reversal of sense and cognition was one not only of priority but also of import.

A Commonsense Philosophy of Taste: Reid's Reply to Hume and Gerard

Thomas Reid opposed Hume's view of how the mind works. Reid believed that the Humean emphasis on ideas and impressions reduced mental operations to objects of thought. Because associationist psychology viewed sensation, memory, and imagination as making representations to the mind, Reid could point out that the emphasis was too much on presence and on discreet units of thought. He viewed the mind instead as the site of innate conceptions and predispositions enabling persons to be and to act in the world. For Reid, the fundamental dimension of thought was belief, not sensation. Vincent Bevilacqua accurately summarized the position of Reid and his allies: "The common sense philosophers . . . see the mind not as a *tabula rasa* void of everything but potential, but as an amalgam of powers, original senses, and propensities which afford immediate perception of self evident truths."[44]

Hume's skepticism had sought to hold in doubt certain fundamental beliefs that form the groundwork of human knowledge (e.g., the principle of universal causation, the uniformity of nature, and belief in the testimony of others). Reid and his allies James Beattie and Dugald Stewart responded that such beliefs were so endemic to our ways of thinking and conceiving the world that to question them was an absurdity, if not impossible.[45] As Stewart noted, the substance of Reid's argument was that "those essential laws of belief to which sceptics have objected, when considered in connection with our scientific reasonings, are implied in every step we take as active beings, and if called into question by any man in his practical concerns would expose him universally to the charge of insanity."[46]

Reid called these laws of belief "commonsense principles," and in them he appealed to a certain "degree of judgment common to men with whom we can converse and conduct business."[47] Reid held that all such persons took for granted certain original principles inherent in human nature and without which all forms of reasoning would be rendered impossible. These included such principles as:

—Whatever begins to exist, must have a cause which produced it.[48]

—Design and intelligence in the cause may be inferred,
with certainty, from the marks or signs of it in the effect.[49]
—The natural world has an existence independent of percipient things.[50]
—The future course of nature will resemble the past.[51]

In identifying such principles, Reid put out of question many of
the very relations Hume made the object of his philosophy.

The perspectives held by Hume and by Reid, then, were
diametrically opposed. What Hume attributed to sensation,
Reid attributed to innate capacities of the mind. For Reid, judgment and other cognitive processes were always at work in all
mental operations like an engine idling, and conception preceded perception and all mental operations. For Hume, sensation and perception preceded all cognitive operations, which
could not occur without the ideas and impressions to which
they gave rise. In terms of rhetoric, a theory of taste based
solely on Humean principles would look exclusively to specific
features of discourse itself (such as the Sublime, the beautiful,
and the ridiculous) to account for discursive affect which would
be immediate and noncognitive. A purely commonsense view
would look to innate capacities and cognitively inbred principles to account for aesthetic response. No subsequent rhetorical
theory relied exclusively on Hume or Reid, however. Instead,
theories of Blair and Campbell incorporated elements of both
the empiricist and commonsense positions.

Reid's theory of taste as articulated in his response to
Hume made these oppositions apparent. Unlike Hume, Reid
was unwilling to locate taste merely in the sensation of pleasure and its attendant sentiments. Reid believed that beauty in
an object arose as much from the object's qualities as from the
percipient's sensation. This followed from the commonsense
principle that there is a natural world independent of perception. As Reid argued, "when a beautiful object is before us, we
may distinguish the agreeable emotion it produces in us, from
the quality of the object which causes that emotion. When I
hear an air in music that pleases me, I say, it is fine, it is excellent. This excellence is not in me; it is in the music. But the
pleasure it gives is not in the music; it is in me."[52] In support

of this view, Reid had recourse to ordinary language; he noted that when we talk about such experiences, we make reference to an excellent air in music or to a delicious taste in food. In so doing, we clearly ascribe the experience we have of the object to some quality in the object itself. Reid furthermore observed that there are many different varieties of beauty—the beauty of a demonstration, of a poem, of a palace, of a fine woman. He noted that we have no way to distinguish such beauties other than by reference to qualities of the objects themselves.[53]

Reid thus felt that the experience of beauty arose, not just from the object itself or from the sentiment of the percipient, but from the relation between the two. In his discussions of novelty, grandeur, and beauty, Reid therefore considered the correlation between the qualities of objects and the ways in which the mind perceives them. Novelty, for example, cannot be a sensation of the mind only; it inevitably depends for its effect on the percipient's past experience. "What is new to one man, may not be so to another; what is new at this moment, may be familiar to the same person some time hence."[54] An unfamiliar object arouses our attention and causes an agreeable exertion of our faculties; we respond as we do because we are so constituted (*a priori*) as to need stimulation and change. With regard to grandeur, Reid believed that all sublime response somehow grew out of the supreme Being whose eternity, immensity, irresistible power, infinite knowledge, and unerring wisdom fill the utmost capacity of the soul.[55] Sublime response to grand objects was thus due to the sign relationship between the creation and its designer to which commonsense philosophy subscribed.

A second opposition between Hume and Reid concerned the origins of taste. Hume, of course, believed that taste developed through cumulative sensory experience, practice, and comparison. Reid responded that aesthetic taste was inborn. Just as the external sense of taste is innate and enables us to discern what is fit for us to eat and to drink, so internal (aesthetic) taste enables us to be pleased with what is most excellent and displeased with the contrary. For this reason, we recognize that persons with distorted or corrupt taste have a natural faculty that has been somehow vitiated or depraved. All those with a natural sense of taste equally recognize and appreciate fine objects and implicitly apply the first principles of aesthetic excellence.[56] Reid did not articulate these aesthetic axioms as he did those of morals and logic.[57] He did note, however, that there was intrinsic beauty in the virtues, graces and muses; that certain moral and intellectual qualities possess original beauty; and that aberrations of nature (such as a face without a nose) are ugly.[58]

A final departure that Reid made from the views of Hume and Gerard concerned the role of judgment in taste. The latter two theorists had made judgment a secondary dimension of taste. Hume viewed judgment as nonessential, and Gerard viewed taste as an internal reflex sense derived from sensation. To this, Reid responded that "in *every* operation of taste, judgment was implied."[59] Reid's position can be represented syllogistically:

> All aesthetic responses evaluate an object [affirm or deny something about it].
> All judgment is simply affirmation or denial.
> Therefore, all aesthetic responses are judgments.[60]

This is to say that all operations of taste are propositional; they are not merely sensations. Rather than saying with Hume "This object gives me pleasure (and therefore is beautiful)," Reid would say "This object is beautiful (because it possesses certain excellent qualities)." In support of his view, Reid again turned to ordinary language: "If it be said that the perception of beauty is merely a feeling in the mind that perceives, without any belief of excellence in the object, the necessary consequence of this opinion is, that when I say 'Virgil's "Georgics" is a beautiful poem,' I mean not to say anything of the poem, but only something concerning myself and my feelings. Why should I use a language that expresses the contrary of what I mean?"[61] Reid concluded by saying that even those philosophers who held that taste was sensation often spoke of beauty as a quality of objects. Their tendency, in Reid's view, was only a sign of human nature's intrinsic belief in the existence of the external world. If there was an external quality perceived by individuals who experienced nature and art, then judgment would have to enter in when they considered the relation between the object and their own response to it.

Reid pointed out that cognition enabled a person to distinguish a given object from others of its genre, to discern the coherence of parts with a whole, to form general notions of excellence and deformity, and to determine whether an object's design was suited to its end. The senses taken alone provided only a gross, indistinct notion of an object, but judgment enabled a person to conceive the object distinctly and thus to affirm or deny its qualities.[62]

Taste therefore entailed cognition. Positive aesthetic judgments arose from recognizing the rightness of the relation between an object and its qualities, not just from a sensory response to it. People responded as they did to beautiful objects because of an innate, universal, and common recognition and appreciation of what was beautiful in nature. This internal sense of beauty provided an origin for a taste standard that could be further improved by education and culture. In his views on taste, Reid opposed the associationists at every turn. He developed a coherent reply to their aesthetics that David O. Robbins has called "the most philosophical and least amateurish [aesthetics] of the whole English eighteenth-century speculation."[63] A rhetorical theory based on the associationism of Hume and Gerard would be noncognitive and emphasize responses triggered by the sensible and sensory features of discourse. (We see this nicely reflected in Campbell's principle that ideas that are made striking, vivid, and lively will have greater appeal and persuasiveness than general or abstract ideas.) A commonsense theory of persuasion, on the other hand, would emphasize judgment's role in the weighing of discursive qualities. Since Hume's and Reid's views on the origin, operations, and nature of taste were so mutually opposed, and since they each represented distinct schools of thought on the matter of taste, one might expect Hugh Blair and George Campbell to develop theories of taste derived from either an associationist or a commonsense orientation. That was not the case, since both rhetoricians eclectically adopted elements from both schools of thought in their theories of rhetoric.

Hugh Blair's Theory of Taste: Something for Everyone

When Blair originally composed his Lectures in 1758–59, Hume's essay on taste had just appeared. And, since Blair was a member of the Select Society of Edinburgh for which Gerard wrote his *Essay on Taste,* one can assume that Blair was familiar with Gerard's views as stated in the first three parts of that work. In a note that Blair appended to his lecture, he referred his readers to these two works, as well as to the theories of taste produced by d'Alembert, Dubos, Burke, and Kames.[64] Since these works were all available to Blair during the first years after he began delivering his lectures in 1759, and since he revised them only minimally later on, one may conclude that the sources Blair cited were the ones he principally used in developing his own views on taste.[65]

Although Reid had not at that time published his writings on taste, Blair did have available to him a commonsense theory in the form of Lord Kames' *Elements of Criticism.*[66] Like Reid, Kames appealed to ordinary language practices to support his views. He argued that there must be a standard of taste somewhere, for people regularly spoke and thought as if one existed. "Do we not talk of a good and a bad taste? Of a right and a wrong taste? . . . Have the foregoing expressions, familiar in all languages and among all peoples, no sort of meaning? This can hardly be: what is universal must have a foundation in nature."[67] Kames went on to argue that in the fine arts there must be an innate and intrinsic taste which precedes all particular aesthetic experience. "Nature is in every particular consistent with herself. . . . We are . . . formed with an uniformity of taste, . . . if uniformity of taste did not prevail, the fine arts could never have made any figure. Thus, upon a sense common to the species, is erected a standard of taste, which without hesitation is apply'd to the taste of every individual."[68]

Kames admitted that there was variability in taste; but he argued that was due to the division of living creatures into classes with varying internal constitutions. "Each class may be conceived to have a common nature, which, in framing the individuals belonging to that class, is taken for a model or standard."[69] (In Kames' theory is manifest an elitism that lies just below the surface of Scottish views on taste but is rarely openly articulated.) To preserve a standard of taste suitable to refined society, the highest standard should not be drawn from "those who depend for food on bodily labour" or those whose "taste [is] corrupted to such a degree as to unqualify them altogether for voting."[70] Kames thus confined the standard of taste to those who had a good natural taste improved by education, reflection, and experience and who had good morals and lived moderately. Kames also included as bases for a taste standard certain principles constituting the sensitive part of human nature, and he noted that acquainting his readers with such principles was the avowed purpose of his work on criticism.

Blair apparently adopted Kames' position regarding a taste standard. He rejected Hume's proposal that the locus of such a standard could be an idealized set of "true judges."

> Now, were there any one person who possessed in full perfection all the powers of human nature, whose internal senses were in every instance exquisite and just, and whose reasoning was unerring and sure, the determinations of such a person concerning beauty, would, beyond doubt, be a perfect standard for the Taste of all others. . . . But as there is no such living standard, no one person to whom all mankind will allow such submission to be due, what is there of sufficient authority to be the standard of the various and opposite Tastes of men?[71]

Blair affirmed instead that taste was "ultimately founded on an internal sense of beauty," that the only taste held to be true and just "coincides with the general sentiments of men" and, furthermore, that one could have recourse to "principles of Taste . . . deeply founded in the human mind."[72] Blair clearly believed that the foundation of taste could be found by reference to commonsense principles accepted by all persons possessing taste in a sound and natural state. Deviant taste could be detected by comparing it with the prevailing general taste. Ascribing taste to an innate capacity intrinsic to all normal persons was consistent with commonsense assumptions about how the mind works in morals, logic, and aesthetics.

The use Blair made of Kames' position on this issue was, for the most part, the only portion of Blair's views on taste that had a commonsense origin. Bevilacqua and others have emphasized these commonsense bases of Blair's theories, but Blair was also influenced by Hume.[73] Hume's essay on taste had appeared just prior to the composition of Blair's lecture; Hume's work was fashionable; Blair had Hume's essay before him; and he used it. As a result, Blair's views on taste consisted of a strange mixture of empiricism and commonsense stances on taste. Blair eclectically borrowed principles from both Hume and his opponent Reid, and his ambivalent footnote on their controversy (to be discussed later in this section) demonstrated Blair's inability to appreciate the fundamental philosophical schism that divided the commonsense and empiricist positions.[74]

Blair's dependence on an empiricist theory of taste was exemplified by his agreement with Hume and Gerard that taste was an internal reflex sense and that aesthetic pleasure was immediate and involuntary. "For nothing can be more clear, than that taste is not resolvable into any such operation of Reason. . . . A beautiful prospect or a fine poem . . . often strike us intuitively, and make a strong impression when we are unable to assign the reasons of our being pleased."[75] The faculty of aesthetic taste was thus viewed as being very much like gustatory taste. Blair viewed reason as important, of course, and he noted, as had Hume and Gerard, that it assisted taste in many of its operations.[76]

Blair also followed Hume closely when he identified attributes contributing to the formation of a fine taste. A fine taste could not be had without possession of "nicer organs" and "finer internal powers."[77] Blair held with Hume that delicacy was an essential attribute of sensibility that enabled one to feel strongly and also to feel accurately. To clarify the discriminating role of taste, Blair made the same comparison with the external sense of taste that Hume had made using the example of the key with the leather thong: "As the goodness of the palate is not tried by strong flavours, but by a mixture of ingredients, where, notwithstanding the confusion, we remain sensible of each; in like manner delicacy of internal Taste appears, by a quick and lively sensibility to its finest, most compounded, or most latent objects."[78]

What had been labelled "practice" in Hume's theory was termed "exercise" by Blair, who agreed that it was of great importance. Blair noted that, just as the external senses of touch, sight, and taste were more finely and highly developed in men who used them daily in their employment, so could the internal sense of taste be developed through study and consideration of "its proper objects."[79] Exercising one's taste could also enable one to perceive aesthetic objects more clearly and distinctly: "When one is only beginning his acquaintance with works of genius, the sentiment which attends them is obscure and confused. He cannot point out the several excellencies or blemishes of a performance which he peruses. . . . But allow him more experience in works of this kind, and his Taste becomes by degrees more exact and enlightened. . . . The mist dissipates which seemed formerly to hang over the object; and he can at length pronounce firmly, without hesitation, concerning it."[80] This passage was taken nearly verbatim from Hume.

Finally, Blair included good sense among the attributes leading to fine taste. As in Hume, this quality was put forward almost as an afterthought, and Blair provided an adumbrated description of its function by noting that it enabled one to decide whether characters, actions, and manners were portrayed in a manner conforming to expectations.

Blair's discussion of taste was therefore heavily indebted to Hume. He made use of most of Hume's attributes of good taste (excluding only freedom from prejudice), lifted certain passages directly from Hume's essay, and invested a good deal in an internal reflex sense view of taste. Blair also borrowed from commonsense stances that supported taste as an innate capacity linked to universal commonsense principles. The result was a rather odd amalgam of empiricist and commonsense aesthetics. Blair's theory was not original, but it was probably not objectionable to his peers and contemporaries, either.

In fact, Blair clearly intended to sit on the fence by pleasing everyone and offending no one. In an explanatory footnote, Blair argued that the differences between Humean and commonsense views of taste were more apparent than real. "They who lay the greatest stress on sentiments and feeling, make no scruple of applying argument and reason to matters of Taste. . . . They . . . who . . . maintain that it is ascertainable by the standard of reason, admit nevertheless, that what pleases universally must on that account be held to be truly beautiful, and that no rules or conclusion concerning . . . Taste can have any just authority if they be found to contradict the general sentiments of men. These two systems, therefore, differ in reality very little from one another."[81] Blair's statement here neglected the deep divergence in philosophical sentiment separating Hume from Kames, Beattie, Reid, Stewart, and other commonsense philosophers who had invested so much faith in the mind's cognitive powers. These theorists had far exceeded Blair in penetrating topics having to do with the arts and with criticism. They focused their attention on the physiological and psychological nature of "the senses." But that kind of inquiry had begun even before the work of Hume and Reid.

Taste in George Campbell's Rhetorical Theory

In 1725, before either Hume or Reid had considered the topic of taste, Francis Hutcheson published *An Inquiry into the Original of our Ideas of Beauty and Virtue*.[82] In this work Hutcheson argued that, alongside the external senses of sight, smell, hearing, taste, and touch, there were internal senses of beauty and of moral virtue. He viewed these senses as operating instantaneously and involuntarily, much like the external senses. An examination of George Campbell's aesthetics reveals a substantial debt to Hutcheson. Considering Hutcheson's theory and comparing it with Hume's and Reid's therefore becomes a necessary preliminary to understanding how taste operated in Campbell's rhetorical theory.

In the first treatise of his work, Hutcheson succinctly summarized the essential elements of his position: "Both [internal and external senses] are natural powers of perception, or determinations of the Mind to receive necessarily certain Ideas from the Presence of Objects. The Internal sense is, a passive Power of receiving ideas of Beauty from all Objects in which there is Uniformity amidst Variety."[83] Hutcheson viewed both internal and external senses as capacities to perceive and experience stimuli in certain ways. Just as hearing (an external sense) enabled one to detect audible sounds, so would "a good ear" (an internal sense) allow one to appreciate a fine harmony. Both acute hearing and a good ear function as predispositions of one's constitution and eventuate in instantaneous and involuntary perceptive response. Along with his description of the internal senses, Hutcheson also indicated his criterion for aesthetic beauty—uniformity amidst variety. The succession of the seasons, the alternation of night and day, the revolutions of planets on their axes, and the variation of plant and animal forms all strike the internal sense of beauty because of the patterns of similarities and differences among them. We do not need to know the cause of the pleasures such beauties afford us: "a Man's Taste may suggest Ideas of Sweets, Acids, Bitters, tho' he be ignorant of the *Forms* of the small Bodys, or their motions, which excite these perceptions in him."[84]

In addition to the absolute beauty perceived in objects of nature, Hutcheson proposed a relative beauty apprehended in objects imitating some original (e.g., the beauty of a mountainous vista versus a painting of the same vista). All statuary, painting, poetry, and other discourse fell into this latter category, being imitations of natural objects and human actions. In the case of imitative works, the sense of beauty would respond to a just representation of the uniformity amidst variety in nature.

In the discursive arts, the role of resemblance was of first importance. "It is by resemblance that Similitudes, Metaphors, and Allegorys are made beautiful, whether either the Subject or the Thing compar'd to it have Beauty or not. . . ."[85] The proportional relationship between the original and its imitation thus gave rise to beauty.

Hutcheson's theory differed from both the commonsense and the Humean views of taste. Reid's theory allowed much more room for cognition. Reid emphasized the role of judgment in aesthetic response; Hutcheson's "inner sense" of taste assumed that such responses were instantaneous and involuntary. In Hutcheson's view, the perception of beauty had an immediacy and inevitability that could arise only from sensation and not from reason.[86] And, whereas Hutcheson attributed sensory pleasure to only one principle—uniformity amidst variety, Reid set forth a number of commonsense principles contributing to aesthetic judgment.

While Hutcheson's theory might seem quite similar to Hume's, it was different in one essential respect. Hutcheson made room in his theory for the beauteous qualities of external objects, whereas Hume emphasized sensory response as the criterion of pleasure. As Dabney Townsend noted in comparing Humean and Hutchesonian aesthetics: "Hutcheson distinguishes an 'original or absolute' beauty from 'comparative or relative' beauty. In Hume's essay this distinction . . . disappears. One can only compare actual judgments. Absolute beauty plays no role. . . . In fact, beauty gives way generally to taste in Hume's essay. The 'facts' Hume has reference to are mostly facts about judges and not about what is judged."[87] Although Hutcheson had emphasized immediate, involuntary response, he actually located his standard of beauty in something external, the uniformity amid variety in nature. This external ascription was incompatible with a Humean skepticism that refused to acknowledge any external cause for aesthetic response.

The aesthetic dimension of George Campbell's *Philosophy of Rhetoric* was an artful mixture of Humean and Hutchesonian aesthetics. Campbell's account of persuasive influence was fundamentally Humean in its view of how the mind works. Campbell nevertheless held to an "internal sense" theory of aesthetic and moral taste, which meant that his explanation of persuasive effects had to take into account their external causes in the nature of the discourse perceived and experienced by an audience.

As I have noted, Campbell considered rhetoric a discursive art with an aesthetic dimension. He divided arts into the useful (e.g., navigation, shipbuilding, medicine) and the fine or elegant (e.g., painting, sculpture, poetry), and he observed that "eloquence and architecture are to be considered as of a mixed nature, wherein utility and beauty have almost equal influence."[88] The discriminating criterion for the fine arts was that their end was "attained by *an accommodation to some internal taste,* so the springs by which alone they can be regulated must be sought for in the nature of the human mind, *and more especially in the principles of the imagination.*"[89] These two passages lead one to conclude that, in Campbell's rhetorical theory, eloquence was a fine art insofar as it made use of the imagination to appeal to an internal sense of beauty. Campbell's description of the process by which this occurred owed much to Hume, while his view of its effects seems to have been drawn from Hutcheson.

Campbell's account of imagination's role in persuasion was explicit:

A passion is most strongly incited by sensation. . . . Next
to the influence of sense is that of memory, the effect of
which upon passion, if the fact be recent, and remembered
distinctly and circumstantially, is almost equal. Next to
influence of memory is that of imagination; by which is
here solely meant the faculty of apprehending what is neither perceived by the senses, nor remembered. Now, as it
is this power of which the orator must chiefly avail himself, it is proper to inquire what those circumstances are,
which will make the ideas he summons up in the imaginations of his hearers, resemble, in lustre and steadiness,
those of sensation and remembrance.[90]

Campbell then reminded his readers that oratory is, in a sense,
painting, and that an orator must exhibit lively and glowing
images of his subject so as to bring his auditors' imaginations
to the point where their representations will impress the mind
as do the stimulations of sense and memory.[91] The orator must
engage the imagination by exhibiting probable, plausible, proximate, and immediate representations of ideas. Only in this
way could passion concerning an absent object be excited by
eloquence "which, by enlivening and invigorating the ideas of
imagination, makes them resemble the impressions of sense
and the traces of memory; and in this respect hath an effect on
the mind similar to that produced by a telescope on sight;
things remote are brought near, things obscure rendered con-
spicuous."[92] It should go almost without saying that this emphasis upon simulating sense impressions and this account of
how persuasion ought to work upon the mind are Humean in
impulse and design.

To describe the effects of such appeals upon the mind,
Campbell turned to Hutcheson and his account of internal
senses. Campbell apparently believed that there were indeed
internal aesthetic and moral senses that functioned very much
like the external senses. Therefore, in making use of the imagination, persuasion appealed to the internal sense of beauty.
Admiration, for example, was a "pleasurable sensation which
instantly ariseth on the perception of magnitude" and "ought
therefore to be numbered among those original feelings of the
mind, which are denominated by some the reflex senses, being

of the same class with a taste for beauty, an ear for music, or our moral sentiments. Now, the immediate view of whatever is directed to the imagination . . . terminates in the gratification of some internal taste. . . ."[93] In discussing sources of evidence somewhat later, Campbell again referred to consciousness of "feelings, whether pleasant or painful, which we derive from what are called the internal senses, and pronounce concerning beauty or deformity, harmony or discord, the elegant or the ridiculous."[94]

Like Hutcheson, Campbell believed that the best means of appealing to this internal sense of beauty was through resemblance. "Nothing contributes more to vivacity than striking resemblances in the imagery, which convey, besides, an additional pleasure of their own."[95] The fancy (as opposed to judgment) receives pleasure when encountering a likeness "which escapes the notice of most people."[96] Comparisons that bring entities together in novel, original, and unanticipated ways appeal to the imagination and invoke pleasure. Campbell therefore endorsed strong, unique resemblances via simile, metaphor, allegory, and even antithesis as means of stimulating the internal sense of beauty and thus appealing to imagination.[97]

The Philosophy of Rhetoric, then, treated eloquence as a fine as well as a useful art. Its function was to enliven ideas in the imagination to such a pitch as to resemble the perceptions of sense and the transcripts of memory.[98] Campbell's requirement that eloquence appeal to the imagination meant that it must have an aesthetic dimension, and thus appeal to taste. The auditors' internal sense of beauty could be stimulated by uncommon resemblances, use of figures, and lively, distinct portrayals of circumstances. Persuasion could only achieve its effect by appealing to the internal sense of taste.

The Roots of Empiricist Aesthetics in the Work of Abbé Dubos

One significant strain in eighteenth-century aesthetics held that the experience of the sublime and the beautiful arose from a complex relation between the aesthetic object and the mind that perceived it. Commonsense philosophers such as

Kames and Reid believed that the mind worked from an innate capacity to experience beautiful objects as beautiful and ugly objects as deformed. This mind also possessed intrinsic cognitive capacities to see parts in terms of a whole and to apply general notions to specific experiences. These philosophers thus viewed conception as prior to all perception and discounted sensory experience as formative of aesthetic pleasure.

Opposed to this view were the sensationists led by Hume.[99] Their aim was to discover an empirically derived standard of taste, and their impulse was to reduce aesthetic response to sensory pleasure or displeasure. They accounted for taste by comparing it to physiological processes (external taste, in particular) or by applying psychological processes of association such as resemblance, contiguity, and causation to aesthetic experience. For them, aesthetic response was passive, instantaneous, and involuntary, like the pleasure caused by a fine wine or the sight of a beautiful landscape. Their locus of taste lay, not in an object's characteristics or the circumstances of aesthetic experience, but in the percipient's sensory response.

But all of these empiricists hedged when they considered the roles of judgment and the standards for taste. Even Hume listed "good sense" among the attributes of his "true judge," noting the need to judge a work's coherence and propriety and admitting that reasoning, if not essential, was "at least requisite" to the operations of taste.[100] Gerard went so far as to acknowledge that "in all operations of taste, judgment is employed; not only in presenting the subjects on which the senses exercise themselves; but also in comparing and weighing the perceptions and decrees of the senses themselves. . . ."[101] Hume hedged further, too, in arguing that delicacy of taste was to be had only through "appeal to [recognized] models and principles."[102] Gerard attempted to extricate Humean theory from this inconsistency by insisting that such principles could themselves be empirically derived. Nevertheless, there was a tacit reluctance here to carry the sensationist viewpoint to its logical conclusion. A pure sensationist would be expected to exclude all cognition from aesthetic judgment, attribute artistic excellence solely to its capacity to cause pleasure in the recipient, and elevate the general public to the status of definitive arbiters of taste. When considering the literati of enlightened Scotland, one looks in vain for a theorist who would take such a position.

In France in the early part of the century, one can find such a person, the Abbé Dubos, whose *Réflexions critiques sur la poësie et sur la peinture* first appeared in 1719.[103] Diplomat, historian, critic, and Secretary of the French Academy, Dubos was a friend and admirer of John Locke and a well-traveled connoisseur of the fine arts. His intention was not to produce a systematic aesthetic theory but rather to give his impressions and opinions, as a man of taste and an amateur, of how the various arts—painting, poetry, music, and drama—were to be judged and compared to one another. The *Réflexions* were impressionistic, episodic, chatty, and verbose. T. M. Mustoxidi has observed that they were in a sense a reaction to the systematic rationalism of Descartes and an effort to discuss aesthetics from a particular empiricist viewpoint: "[Dubos] is . . . an empiricist, a sensualist, but first of all and to avoid grand words, Dubos accepts facts and attempts, not to adapt them to aprioristic hypotheses, but simply to explain them by assenting to them insofar as possible."[104/b]

Saisselin has noted that the *Réflexions* "are indispensable reading for those who would understand eighteenth-century French and other European aesthetics. . . ."[105] Saisselin further observed that Dubos was used "by everyone," even though he was often not cited, footnoted, or acknowledged. Peter Jones has demonstrated that Hume's essay on the standard of taste was very heavily indebted to Dubos, so much so that Hume's reluctance to publish his own essay may have been due to recognition of its dependence on the French critic.[106] Certain elements of Hume's essay do indeed appear to have been taken directly from Dubos, namely his emphasis upon pleasure and sentiment, on the need for good organs, and his insistence on practice in comparing works of art. Gerard, too, relied upon Dubos, citing him more frequently than any other French critic.[107] Blair and Campbell had also read Dubos. In his lecture

---

b. [Dubos] est . . . un empiriste, un sensualiste, mais avant tout et pour éviter les grands mots, Dubos accepte les faits et essaie, non pas de les adapter à des hypothèses aprioristiques, mais simplement de les expliquer en s'y soumettant dans la mesure du possible.

on taste, Blair referred his readers to Dubos' writing on the same subject, and he also cited the French author on the role of music in ancient tragedies and on the effects of climate on genius.[108] Campbell twice cited Dubos' view that the mind seeks diversion and abhors languor and ennui.[109] Dubos' more substantial contribution to Blair's theory of taste, however, arose from Blair's reliance upon Hume who in turn relied on Dubos.

Even if it were not for this considerable evidence of Dubos' influence, he would be of interest here because his views on taste took the form of an empiricist approach carried to its logical conclusion. Unlike his Scottish counterparts, Dubos did not shy away from an empirical standard of taste; in his theory what pleases is beautiful and what does not, is not. The final arbiter of taste is the general public, not the *gens de métier* or practicing critics or an educated elite. Dubos wasted no time, either, in deprecating judgment's role in aesthetic response and in denigrating artistic rules and principles.

Dubos' conceptions of artistic production and reception were mechanistic and physiological. For him, artistic genius "consists in a favorable arrangement of the brain's organs, in the good structure of each of these organs, as in the quality of the blood, which inclines it to ferment during work so as to produce abundant [animal] spirits for the activities useful to the functions of the imagination."[110/c] In eloquence and poetry, the purpose of such mental activity is to provide vivid portrayals and depictions of human action so that readers and auditors can imagine the passions and sentiments portrayed. The poet or orator must "find expressions suited to render these passions sensible and to cause these sentiments to be felt."[111/d] For Dubos, as for Hume and Campbell, the aesthetic value of any discursive work arises from its capacity to make its audiences feel the experiences and sentiments portrayed, much as they

---

c. consiste en un arrangement heureux des organes du cerveau, dans la bonne conformation de chacun de ces organes, comme dans la qualité du sang, laquelle le dispose à fermenter durant le travail, de maniere qu'il fournisse en abondance des esprits aux aux [sic] ressorts qui servent aux fonctions de l'imagination.

d. trouver les expressions propres à rendre ces passions sensibles & à faire deviner ces sentimens.

would if they were in the actual situation. This imitative, representational quality itself was what furnished the aesthetic pleasure that came from the work.

The way to judge any artistic work, then, was to determine whether it pleased its audience. "Does the work please, or doesn't it? Is the work generally good or bad? These amount to the same thing."[112/e] In Dubos' aesthetics, this response was not a complex one requiring a certain configuration of the object's qualities and the percipient's disposition (as it was in Hume).[113] Rather, the desired response was simple, sensory pleasure. The temptation to compare the aesthetic taste with the gustatory was irresistible: "Does one reason in order to know whether the ragout is good or bad? . . . One does nothing of the sort. There is in us a sense made to recognize whether the cook has performed according to the rules of his art. One tastes the ragout and, even without knowing the rules, one recognizes whether it is good. In the same way are works of talent and tableaux made to please us by touching us."[114/f] Clearly, Dubos did not believe that recourse to artistic rules and principles was necessary for artistic response. Instead, he argued that there was in us "a sixth sense" that makes judgments based on immediate impressions. This sixth sense "is in short what is commonly called sentiment."[115/g] By "sentiment" Dubos meant "feeling or sensation." In Hume, the same term had various meanings. As Jones noted, "the ambiguity in the French term *sentiment,* deplored by French and English writers alike, is precisely mirrored in Hume's term 'sentiment,' by which he sometimes means 'emotion, passion' and sometimes 'judgment, opinion'; indeed, for him, the term treacherously covers both feeling and thought, which are otherwise often kept apart by the notions of impression and idea."[116]

As Jones' observation implies, Dubos and Hume apparently

---

e. L'ouvrage plaît-il ou ne plaît-il pas? L'ouvrage est-il bon on [sic] mauvais en géneral? C'est la même chose.

f. Raisonne-t-on, pour savoir si le ragoût est bon ou s'il est mauvais?. . . . On n'en fait rien. Il est en nous un sens fait pour connoître si le Cuisinier a opéré suivant les régles de son art. On goûte le ragoût & même sans savoir ces régles, on connoît s'il est bon. Il en est de même en quelque maniere des ouvrages d'esprit & des tableaux faits pour nous plaire en nous touchant.

g. est enfin ce qu'on appelle communément le sentiment.

disagreed about the role of judgment in responses to art and discourse. Hume had given a nod to judgment and reasoning by including the criteria of good sense and delicacy of taste in forming the true judge. Dubos aggressively opposed incorporation of judgment and, in fact, sought to subvert it to sentiment. "Reasoning should intervene in the judgment we make of a poem or tableau only to account for the decisions of sentiment and to explain what faults prevent its being pleased and what ornaments render it capable of being engaged."[117/h] Sentiment renders the decision about a work; reasoning and judgment only justify it after the fact. In describing the orator's task, Dubos again effected the same means/ends reversal: "His aim is . . . to lead us to his sentiment through the force of his reasonings. . . ."[118/i] The *telos* of all art was to effect sentiment, and judgment played no immediate role in this process.

If sentiment, rather than artistic rules and principles, was the means of deciding about a work, then the general public—the "man in the street," so to speak—could serve as the final arbiter of taste. Dubos took this position, although he did equivocate somewhat by arguing that the "public" to which he referred should include only those persons who were well read, attended plays, viewed art works, and discussed aesthetic matters so as to form a *goût de comparaison*.[119] No particular education or training was required however, knowledge of principles being unnecessary. Dubos also excluded artists, critics, and *gens de métier* as arbiters of a taste standard. He believed that the tastes of such persons might be jaded or that they might overvalue what they personally believed to be important. Critics, in particular, were prone to make reasoned judgments rather than rely on sentiment. The members of the general public were uniquely qualified because they relied upon sentiment and responded through an interior movement that only they could explain. Dubos argued that it was to their reactions that one should look to judge a work's impact: "The

---

h. Le raisonnement ne doit donc intervenir dans le jugement que nous portons sur un poëme ou sur un tableau, que pour rendre raison de la décision du sentiment & pour expliquer quelles fautes l'empêchent de plaire & quels sont les agréments qui le rendent capable d'attacher.

i. Sa derniere fin est . . . de nous amener à son sentiment par la force de ses raisonnemens. . . .

theatre pit, without knowing the rules, judges a play as well as professionals. . . . As soon as the movements of their hearts that operate mechanically, come to be expressed by their gesture and countenance, they become a touchstone which allows one to know distinctly whether the principal merit in the work is lacking or not. . . ."[120/j]

Dubos was more than simply a precursor of Hume and Gerard. As a critic who unflinchingly promoted sentiment and feeling to the exclusion of reasoning and judgment, and as one who disparaged rules and principles and democratized the taste standard by placing it with the general public, Dubos instantiated the empiricist position. He was a sensationist *extraordinaire* and he carried the implications of that position to their logical conclusion. In his absolute rejection of judgment as having a role in taste, he differed from all of the British theorists who followed him. Any eloquence based on Dubos' theory would have to make extensive use of lively and glowing images. Dubos would very likely have agreed with the major principles of Campbell's *Philosophy of Rhetoric* while at the same time doubting whether Campbell needed to articulate them.

In his *Réflexions,* too, Dubos viewed all the arts as functioning similarly, and that similarity arose from what Dubos believed was their profoundly rhetorical nature. "The sublime in poetry and painting is to touch and to please as that of eloquence is to persuade."[121/k] But, as Basil Munteano has argued, Dubos hardly separated the two domains. "It indeed appears that the two arts differ in their finality—*to touch* and *to please* on one hand, *to persuade* on the other. Unfortunately, ends and means are inextricably mixed together. In fact, for poetry what is it *to touch* and *to please* if not to communicate to another these states of the soul, and thus in the same way to persuade, as in eloquence? Inversely, eloquence persuades only by dint of *pleasing* and *touching—delectare, movere*—assuming thus as

----

j. Le Parterre, sans savoir les régles, juge d'une piéce de théatre aussibien que les gens du métier. . . . Dès que les mouvements de leur coeur qui opére mécaniquement, viennent à s'exprimer par leur geste & par leur contenance, ils deviennent une pierre de touche laquelle donne à connoître distinctement si le mérite principal manque ou non dans l'ouvrage. . . .

k. Le Sublime de la Poësie & de la Peinture est de toucher & de plaire, comme celui de l'Eloquence est de persuader.

instrument the proper objective assigned by Dubos to poetry and painting."[122/1] Munteano has here identified the precise reason why taste was so important to the rhetoricians of the eighteenth century who believed that it was only by aesthetic means that suasive ends could be achieved.

Conclusion

Of the French belletrists' views on taste, those of Dubos were most frequently cited by the Scots. Hume, in particular, was attracted to Dubos' emphasis on sensory stimulation and pleasure when accounting for aesthetic effect. Inspired by Hume, Gerard and Campbell converted their attraction to empiricism into theories of discursive influence that emphasized clarity, ingenuity, specificity, and use of uncommon resemblances as means of triggering immediate and involuntary aesthetic pleasure. Influenced as they were by the British analytic tradition, the Scots nevertheless could not set aside entirely the role of cognition in aesthetic response. Smuggled into Hume's theory as "good sense," cognition took the form of judgment in assessing a work's propriety and coherence, and in Gerard's views on taste cognition involved applying associationist principles to judge a work's effect.

Foremost among the Scottish belletrists, too, were commonsense theorists Kames, Reid, and Stewart. These men made the theory of aesthetic reception a venue for a struggle between associationist and commonsense views of how the mind works. Whereas a Humean would argue that the mind's delight in novelty, magnitude, uniformity, and vivacity results from sensory stimulation and cumulative experience, a commonsense theorist would respond that such qualities resonate with an innate capacity of the mind to recognize and appreciate external beauty. Commonsense theorists also emphasized the

---

1. Il y apparaît bien, certes, que les arts différent dans leur finalité,— *toucher* et *plaire* d'une part, *persuader* de l'autre. Par malheur, fins et moyens s'y mêlent inextricablement. Qu'est-ce, en effect, pour la poésie, que *toucher* et *plaire,* sinon communiquer à autrui ces états d'âme, et donc, de quelque manière, *persuader,* tout comme l'éloquence? Inversement, l'éloquence ne persuade . . . qu'à force de *plaire* et de *toucher*—*delectare, movere,* assumant ainsi comme instrument le propre objectif que Du Bos assigne à la poésie, à la Peinture. . . .

cognitive processes that occur when discursive effects are weighed and compared with each other, past experience, and anticipated pleasure.

The Scots' preoccupation with taste led them to consider systematically the processes of reception. Because their view of rhetoric was managerial rather than epistemic, Blair, Smith, and Campbell emphasized the aesthetic dimensions of receptive influence. More than the rhetorics of any other time, theirs were concerned with the faculties of receptive judgment, uniformity of taste, standards of taste, and whether taste was improvable. The Scottish belletrists' writings on taste were highly speculative and lacked coherence. Nevertheless, they provided the sixth canon's receptive pole and reflected the divergent and incongruous strains in eighteenth-century Scottish thought.

Conclusion

In sixteenth-century France, Peter Ramus removed invention from rhetoric and left to the study and teaching of the art only style and delivery. In the century that followed. René Descartes dealt rhetorical invention a further blow by advocating mathematical proofs to the exclusion of all forms of probabilistic reasoning. By the late seventeenth century, rhetorical logic had been displaced; the commonplaces were viewed only as devices for amplification, and stasis theory was considered irrelevant to occasions for speaking in France. The fate of rhetorical invention was made apparent in French belletristic rhetorics such as Lamy's *L'Art de parler* and Fénelon's *Dialogues sur l'éloquence*. The former emphasized syllogistic proofs based on clear and distinct ideas (a Cartesian model), while the latter neglected invention altogether.

During the Enlightenment, French and Scottish rhetorics turned to a managerial view of rhetoric that distinguished the discovery of knowledge through reasoning from communication of content to others. Invention was eclipsed as Enlightenment rhetoricians focused on stylistic management or conduct of a discourse. French rhetorics displaced invention because of Cartesian and Ramistic influence, while the Scots de-emphasized invention because associationist psychology itself de-emphasized cognition and with it processes of designing argumentation.

While concern for invention and the production of discourse receded, intense interest in the problem of receptive competence emerged to take its place. Late seventeenth-century France had witnessed the demise of neoclassicism and with it the supposed rules and principles governing aesthetic judgment. There was a need to develop new, empirically-grounded principles to take their place. Furthermore, aesthetic sensitivity was viewed as a sign of social competence and education. In eighteenth-century France and in Scotland, the topic of taste attracted the attention of all literate readers. In rhetoric, Fénelon, Rollin, Blair, and Smith all sought to make explicit the aesthetic dimensions of discourse that facilitated its reception and its persuasiveness.

Their efforts eventuated in the sixth canon—a fusion of aesthetics and culturally-based psychology. The sixth canon was comprised of three dimensions parallelling the logical, pathetic, and ethical dimensions of Aristotelian rhetoric. The first, or "logical" dimension, preserved cognition and intellection insofar as they persisted at all during this period and took the form of *vraisemblance* or propriety. Recipients judging a work's appropriateness weighed its plausibility in light of their own past experience as well as the work's conformity to cultural conventions and acceptable modes of expression. Works violating readers' and listeners' expectations of what was natural and suitable would fail to achieve identification and thus fail to be persuasive.

The sixth canon's pathetic dimension was exemplified in the Sublime. As a "pleasurable sensation which instantly ariseth on perception of magnitude," the Sublime bypassed all cognition, since belletrists emphasized the sudden, awestruck nature of sublime response.[1] The Sublime signaled belletrism's emphasis on emotion and reception as the sublime response was treated through the dual lenses of associationism and faculty psychology. Unlike Aristotelian *pathos* which was based on the general psychological makeup of an audience (as seen through the eyes of the speaker), the belletristic Sublime was invested in individual response (as experienced by the listener).

Finally (and this may stretch the Aristotelian parallel somewhat), the sixth canon's third dimension, taste, was treated in ways that made the concept analogous to *ethos*. Whereas Aristotelian *ethos* arose from the credibility of the speaker and the speaker's persona as discursively constructed, taste depended upon the perceptive capacity and competence of the recipient. Rhetorics focusing on production might consider the origin and dimensions of *ethos;* rhetorics emphasizing reception (i.e., the belletristic rhetorics) carefully analyzed the origins and nature of taste. They could only do so by considering how discourse worked upon the psyche, and thus theories of taste became the venue for struggles between associationism and commonsense philosophy.

The Scottish belletrists viewed discourse as a fabric made up of elements that, taken separately, had certain kinds of effects. These elements included the beautiful, the Sublime, the picturesque, the vehement, and the ridiculous. The Scots subscribed more or less to associationist psychology, and they viewed the mind as combining perceptions and impressions. For them, rhetorical affect was the result of assimilating concrete, particular experience. Smith, Campbell, and Blair aimed to identify these individual discursive elements and to explain their effects. In the course of providing their psychological and physiological explanations, the Scottish belletrists sought to develop general principles of human communication and human nature and thus to develop a "philosophy of rhetoric."

Two of the period's most popular rhetorics—Blair's *Lectures on Rhetoric and Belles Lettres* and Campbell's *Philosophy of Rhetoric*—illustrated the various ways in which the Scottish belletrists went about developing a theory of receptive competence. Blair's treatise was a loosely-woven pedagogy that aimed to instruct its reader on the basic elements of good prose style and the rudiments of criticism. Blair treated propriety as a dimension of style, the avoidance of ill-chosen words that violated standards of good English usage. Like his French predecessor Boileau, Blair considered the Sublime a discursive paradigm characterized by immediate emotive response as the listener or reader was struck with awe and the grandeur of the thought conveyed. Blair's discussion of the Sublime overlooked the contributions of his immediate predecessors, borrowed heavily from Boileau's seventeenth-century translation of the pseudo-Longinian treatise, and foreshadowed the interest in the ineffable and mysterious that was to characterize Romanticism.

In belletristic rhetorics, the topic of taste became the locus for criticism and judgment of eloquence and oratory. Blair's treatment of taste was a mishmash of commonsense principles and Humean empiricism. Unlike Hume, Blair held that there were commonsense principles of taste accepted by all persons possessing taste in a sound, natural state, and he set out to articulate them. However, like Hume he disparaged reason's role in aesthetic judgment and emphasized the significance of percipient experience and sound organs of perception. Blair's final position on the role of cognition and judgment in taste was very unclear.

In regard to the sixth canon, Campbell's aim and procedure were strikingly different from Blair's. Campbell was an analyst, and he intended to discover the principles of human nature by studying how rhetoric operated upon the human mind. Campbell made use of the Sublime in delimiting his theory of genres (enlighten the understanding, please the imagination, move the passions, and influence the will). For Campbell, the Sublime was primarily intellective, the use of subtle, uncommon, and ingenious resemblances that strike the recipient with their originality and grandeur. For Campbell, the Sublime demarcated the element of discourse appealing to the imagination; it identified the arena in which oratory was most like poetry.

Campbell defined propriety both in terms of linguistic and social convention. Linguistically, propriety was a dimension of linguistic purity, the avoidance of malapropisms and of words and dialects that violated good English usage. Campbell's discussion of linguistic impropriety was much more finely tuned than Blair's, for Campbell viewed linguistic correctness as a vital element in the aesthetic appeal of discourse, and thus in its rhetorical effectiveness. In its social dimension, propriety resembled the French conception of *vraisemblance,* whether events and descriptions portrayed by an orator conformed to the audience's prior experience of what was normal and natural in a given circumstance. Violation of audience expectations would render discourse implausible and thus rhetorically ineffective. Observance of propriety and use of vivid, noble, and uncommon images meant that eloquence was, in a sense, a fine art. Eloquence that summoned up vivid images would cause an effect resembling sensation and evoking memories of sensation (thus setting into motion association of ideas). For Campbell, a person of taste possessed an internal sense of beauty that responded to discourse that made events, characters, and phenomena proximate, plausible, and immediate.

The entire development of a theory of receptive competence was based on the assumption that a theorist's personal predilections could ground general truths about aesthetic experience. Belletristic aesthetics were "empirical" only in the sense that they were based on the critic's response to discursive elements (as approved and accepted by his readers).[2] Nonetheless, the projects undertaken in belletristic rhetorics (developing a taxonomy of aesthetic elements, spelling out dimensions of discursive propriety, and considering bases of receptive competence) are not fully developed elsewhere in the rhetorical tradition. Taken together, they constitute an extension of the tradition, a sixth canon of rhetoric.

In developing the sixth canon, the Scottish belletrists turned to their French predecessors for elements and ideas that contributed to their theories.[3] From Fénelon they drew the idea that the substance of a subject and the manner of its expression should proportionately correspond to each other. They also agreed with the French critic that the style in which a speaker expressed himself should conform to his character and to the situation at hand. Fénelon's own perspicuous, flowing, unselfconscious style was particularly admired by the Scots.

They turned, too, to Boileau, whose French translation of the pseudo-Longinian *On the Sublime* remained influential throughout the eighteenth century. Boileau had set out to dissociate the Sublime from the sublime style, to invest it with significance as a critical paradigm, and to use it to disparage baroque and overfigured discourse. The Sublime was inherently appealing to the Scots with their interest in emotive response, aesthetic judgment, and stylistic perspicuity. In the hands of the Scots, the Bolevian Sublime was stripped of its neoclassical elements and became itself a chameleon. It was ascribed by various theorists to emotive response, natural grandeur, or simplicity of expression, and it was given materialist, linguistic, or aesthetic attributes depending on the theory in which it was housed.

In the French critic Dubos, the Scots saw the logical extension of the empiricism they found so attractive. Dubos equated a work's artistic merit with its ability to cause pleasure. He converted aesthetic taste into a "sixth sense," a sentiment by which aesthetic qualities could be appreciated by anyone with a modicum of prior experience. Dubos' theory appealed to the Scots who were familiar with Francis Hutcheson's "reflex sense" theory that postulated seven senses—the five external senses, plus an aesthetic sense and a moral sense. Comparison of aesthetic taste to gustatory taste was also compatible with the sensationist psychology to which Hume subscribed. The Scots thus made use of Dubos' views on the effects of languor on the mind and the qualities of aesthetic response. Dubos' views on the origin of aesthetic pleasure were borrowed by Hume and through him by Gerard and by Campbell.

The process of borrowing parts of earlier theories and incorporating them into later theories was not unproblematic, however. Belletristic rhetorics were heterogenous and complex, sometimes even to the point of incoherence. Influenced by empiricism, skepticism, associationism, and commonsense philosophy, the rhetorics of Blair and Campbell were amalgams of diverse strands of thinking. Occasionally, an author of the period managed to synthesize diverse positions into an epistemologically satisfying theory. (Gerard's *Essay on Taste* might be an example.) More often, authors tried to meld together positions that were epistemologically oxymoronic. These authors' work on the sixth canon often shows this tendency to combine positions that make strange bed partners.

For example, Blair began his discussion of taste by attempting to found taste on an internal, universal sense of beauty. He drew this position from Kames' commonsense principle that there is an innate sense of the beautiful in human nature. Blair then immediately turned to Hume and rested his criteria for good taste on empiricist grounds (good organs, delicacy, exercise, and good sense). Hume had held that taste was not innate, that it was attained through experience; Reid insisted that we come into the world with an inherent capacity to apprehend beauty. Blair's internal sense idea of taste was fundamentally incompatible with his Humean account of the acquisition of taste, yet Blair himself seemed quite unaware of the contradiction.

Campbell combined empiricist and commonsense principles simultaneously into his *Philosophy of Rhetoric* and did so in such a way that contemporary critics continue to disagree about the relative weight of Hume's and Reid's respective influence on Campbell's work.[4] In regard to what I have called the sixth canon, there was a latent incompatibility at work in Campbell's aesthetics. Like Hume, Campbell held that the mind was affected by sensation or by images that simulate sensation. Thus one would expect Campbell to agree with Hume that aesthetic sensitivity is based on cumulative external experience. Instead, Campbell subscribed to Hutcheson's "reflex sense theory"—which assumed that moral sense and aesthetic sense (a taste for beauty) were no less innate than sight, touch, gustatory taste, smell, and hearing. Campbell's theory thus implied simultaneously that aesthetic sensibility was acquired through experience and that it was innate.

Manifestations of the Sublime in eighteenth-century rhetorics also illustrated similar problems of adoption and adaptation. For Boileau and for Blair, the Sublime was a critical touchstone invoking instantaneous, powerful, emotive responses. Sublimity was located in the recipient who was irresistibly swept along by the power and grandeur of a work's artistry. For Priestley, the Sublime could be reduced to qualities of the objects portrayed. Priestley's view was materialistic and scientistic, considering the Sublime as a communicated element equivalent to the novel, the beautiful, and the picturesque. For Campbell, the analyst and systematizer, the Sublime was useful in demarcating a particular kind of discourse—that which was addressed to the imagination. Appeals to the imagination as exemplified by the Sublime with its great and noble images were essential in Campbell's system to the arousal of the passions and to moving the will, and so Campbell was preoccupied with its sources and effects. He attributed the Sublime to perception of uncommon and arresting resemblances.

The Sublime served a different purpose of each of these authors. Blair saw the Sublime as elevating a certain kind of discourse to a privileged position and as illustrating for his students a desirable standard of taste. Priestley described the effects of the Sublime by using principles of Hartleian association of ideas, thus demonstrating their usefulness to his satisfaction. And Campbell used the Sublime to differentiate one genre of discourse from others. In all three of these theories the Sublime was paradigmatic, although the phenomena to which it was applied differed. For Blair the Sublime was primarily a taste standard; for Priestley it was an exemplar of materialist affect; and for Campbell it was a means to make distinctions among genres. Through all of these changes the Sublime retained its ability to "distend the imagination with some vast conception, and quite ravish the soul."[5]

Eighteenth-century Scottish rhetorics approached study of persuasive influence from a perspective entirely different from the neoclassical rhetorics that preceded them. They were not concerned with production, source credibility, invention, or the particular rhetorical situation. Instead, they emphasized reception, the origins and development of taste, and the aesthetic dimensions of discourse as generalized phenomena. The Scottish rhetorics were particularly committed to the inductive study of experience and of discourse as a sign of how the mind operates. Like modern hermeneuticists, the belletrists were concerned with second-order reference, with the senses in which experiences and narratives portrayed in a text resonate with the experiences and lives of the text's audience. The belletristic rhetorics have been ill-served by studies that view them through a neoclassical lens. The present study has instead considered them on their own terms, as products of the intellectual climate of the Enlightenment and as reflections of a desire to improve taste and discernment in Scottish culture.

Notes

Introduction

1. Adam Smith, *Lectures on Rhetoric and Belles Lettres,* ed. J. C. Bryce (Oxford: Clarendon, 1983).
2. David Daiches, Peter Jones, and Jean Jones, eds., *A Hotbed of Genius: The Scottish Enlightenment* (Edinburgh: Edinburgh University Press, 1986), 109.
3. Smith, 138.
4. Smith, 25. As I will explain in chapter 2, sympathy in Smith's theory is a sort of empathy or "fellow feeling" with another person. Observing propriety in style and expression enables readers and listeners to identify more easily with the speaker or author and what he or she says. See Patricia R. Spence, "Sympathy and Propriety in Adam Smith's Rhetoric," *Quarterly Journal of Speech* 60 (1974): 92–99.
5. Brian Vickers, *In Defence of Rhetoric* (Oxford: Clarendon Press, 1988), 296.
6. James L. Golden and Edward P. J. Corbett, *The Rhetoric of Blair, Campbell, and Whately* (New York: Holt, 1968), 8, 24.
7. Hugh Blair, *Lectures on Rhetoric and Belles Lettres,* ed. Harold F. Harding, 2 vols. (Carbondale: Southern Illinois University Press, 1965).
8. Golden and Corbett, 25.
9. Golden and Corbett, 8–9; Harding's "Introduction," viii.
10. Blair, 1:5.
11. A publication history and summary of John Ward's lectures (*A System of Oratory* [London, 1759] is provided in Wilbur Samuel Howell, *Eighteenth-Century British Logic and Rhetoric* (Princeton: Princeton University Press, 1971), 89–124. Also, see John Lawson, *Lectures concerning Oratory,* ed. E. Neal Claussen and Karl R. Wallace (Carbondale: Southern Illinois University Press, 1972).
12. Nancy S. Struever, "The Conversable World," in *Rhetoric and the Pursuit of Truth: Language Change in the Seventeenth and Eighteenth Centuries* (Los Angeles: Clark Memorial Library, 1985), 80. This book was written with Brian Vickers. Here Struever was

speaking of David Hume, but her observation applies equally well to Hume's contemporaries.

13. Francis Hutcheson, *An Inquiry into the Original of our Ideas of Beauty and Virtue,* 4th ed. (London: Midwinter, 1738; Reprint, Westmead: Gregg, 1969), xiii.

14. In addition to Smith's and Blair's lectures previously cited, see George Campbell, *The Philosophy of Rhetoric,* ed. Lloyd F. Bitzer (Carbondale: Southern Illinois University Press, 1988).

15. Walter John Hipple, *The Beautiful, the Sublime, and the Picturesque* (Carbondale: Southern Illinois University Press, 1957), x–xi.

16. George A. Kennedy, *Classical Rhetoric and its Christian and Secular Tradition from Ancient to Modern Times* (Chapel Hill: University of North Carolina Press), 15–16.

17. Golden and Corbett, 8; Harding's "Introduction," xxi; and Howell, 519–20.

18. On René Rapin, see Howell, 520–21; Bernard Lamy, *De l'art de parler* (Paris: Pralard, 1676); François de Fénelon *Lettre à l'Académie,* ed. Ernesta Caldarini (Geneva: Librairie Droz, 1970); his *Dialogues sur l'éloquence* (Paris: Garnier Frères, 1866); and Charles Rollin, *De la manière d'enseigner et d'étudier les Belles Lettres,* 4 vols. (Lyon: Rusand, 1819).

19. Dominique Bouhours, *Entretiens d'Ariste et d'Eugène,* ed. René Radouant (1671; Reprint, Paris: Bossard, 1920); and his *La Manière de bien penser dans les ouvrages d'esprit* (1715; Reprint, Brighton: University of Sussex, 1971).

20. Nicolas Boileau-Despréaux, *Oeuvres complètes,* ed. Antoine Adam (Paris: Editions Gallimard, 1966).

21. Jean-Baptiste Dubos, *Réflexions critiques sur la poésie et sur la peinture,* 3 vols. (Utrecht: E. Neaulme, 1732–36).

22. Ernst Cassirer, *The Philosophy of the Enlightenment,* trans. Fritz C. A. Koelin and James P. Pettegrove (Princeton: Princeton University Press, 1951), 303.

23. This view was attributed to Smith by Dugald Stewart in his "Account of the Life and Writings of Adam Smith, LL.D." in *Essays on Philosophical Subjects by the Late Adam Smith* (1795; Reprint, Hildesheim: Verlag, 1982), xvi.

24. René Descartes, *Les Passions de l'âme* (Paris: Gallimard, 1988), 159–66.

25. Dubos, 2:8. My translation.

26. Jean-Paul Sermain, *Rhétorique et roman au dix-huitième siècle* (Oxford: Alden Press, 1985), 16. My translation.

27. Bitzer's "Introduction" to Campbell's *Philosophy,* xii; Howell,

583–94; and Vincent M. Bevilacqua, "Philosophical Origins of George Campbell's *Philosophy of Rhetoric*," *Speech Monographs* 32 (1965), 2–9.

28. Bitzer's "Introduction" to Campbell, xxix–xxxv.
29. Campbell, 3.
30. Douglas W. Ehninger, "George Campbell and the Revolution in Inventional Theory," *Southern Speech Journal* 15 (1950), 275.
31. See, for example, Bevilacqua, "Philosophical Origins," 7; and his "Philosophical Assumptions Underlying Hugh Blair's *Lectures on Rhetoric and Belles Lettres*," *Western Speech Journal* 31 (1967), 161.
32. Golden and Corbett, 14.
33. Lloyd F. Bitzer, "Hume's Philosophy in George Campbell's *Philosophy of Rhetoric*," *Philosophy and Rhetoric* 2 (1969), 160.
34. Howell, 670.
35. Howell, 441–47.
36. Howell, 721 and 739. Both references are to the same two pages.
37. Howell, *Poetics, Rhetoric, and Logic: Studies in the Basic Disciplines of Criticism* (Ithaca, NY: Cornell University Press, 1975), 138.
38. Bevilacqua, "The Rhetorical Theory of Henry Home, Lord Kames" (Ph.D. diss., University of Illinois, 1961), 38.
39. Bevilacqua, "The Rhetorical Theory," 65.
40. Bevilacqua, "Lord Kames's Theory of Rhetoric," *Speech Monographs* 30 (1963), 314.
41. Bevilacqua, "Lord Kames's Theory of Rhetoric," 316–18.
42. Bevilacqua, "Philosophical Origins," 1–12.
43. Bevilacqua, "Philosophical Assumptions," 150–64.
44. Bevilacqua, "Philosophical Origins," 9.
45. Dennis R. Bormann, "George Campbell's *Cura Prima* on Eloquence—1758," *Quarterly Journal of Speech* 74 (1988), 48.
46. Campbell, 388–89.
47. Keith Marshall, "France and the Scottish Press, 1700–1800," *Studies in Scottish Literature* 13 (1978), 8; see also Richard B. Sher, *Church and University in the Scottish Enlightenment* (Edinburgh: Edinburgh University Press, 1985), 29. For an account of Scottish influence on French thought, see James Manns, "The Scottish Influence on French Aesthetic Thought," *Journal of the History of Ideas* 49 (1988), 633–51.
48. On the publication dates of translations of Lamy, Rapin, and Rollin, respectively, see Howell, 503, 524, and 532. On the publication dates of Fénelon's *Letter to the French Academy* and his *Dialogues on Eloquence* in English, see Howell's translation of

Fénelon's Dialogues on Eloquence (Princeton: Princeton University Press, 1951), 49. And on the translation of Dubos, see Peter Jones, *Hume's Sentiments: Their Ciceronian and French Context* (Edinburgh: Edinburgh University Press, 1982), 93.

49. D. D. Raphael in Daiches, *A Hotbed of Genius,* 71.

50. See John M. Lothian's edition of Adam Smith's *Lectures on Rhetoric and Belles Lettres* (London: Nelson, 1963), 8, 70, 72, 127, 140.

51. This text of Smith's lectures is taken from the notes of two student copyists who evidently recorded them from memory in 1762–63. Howell (pp. 544–45) spoke of the unreliability of this version of the lectures. The students might have distorted what Smith said; the notes might be third hand, having been copied from other notes; and duplication of the notes into printed form might have introduced additional errors. Howell's cautionary observations seem well founded, particularly in regard to the French authors studied here.

52. Harding's "Introduction" to Blair's *Lectures,* ix.

53. I made a hand count of citations of French authors in the treatises of Smith, Blair, and Campbell. (The indexes to these works are not reliable.) Of the three, Blair cited a larger number of French sources and did so more frequently than Smith or Campbell. Cited most frequently were Boileau, Bossuet, Fénelon, Massillon, and Voltaire. Blair's reliance on Rollin was discussed in my "Charles Rollin's *Traité* and the Rhetorical Theories of Smith, Campbell, and Blair," *Rhetorica* 3 (1985), 61–62.

54. Campbell, 232, 235, and 395.

55. In order of citation, Campbell, 3; 113, 129; 120–21; and 6, 349.

56. Campbell, 82.

57. Aristotle *The Rhetoric* 1355b.

Chapter 1: Lamy's *L'Art de Parler* and the Eclipse of Invention

1. Balthasar Gibert, *Le Rhétorique, ou les règles de l'éloquence* (Paris: Thiboust, 1730), 10. Unless otherwise noted, all translations from the French in this chapter are mine.

2. *Encyclopédie, ou Dictionnaire raisonné des sciences, des arts et des métiers,* s.v. "Gibert, Balthasar." See also Gibert's *Jugemens des savans sur les auteurs qui ont traité de la rhetorique* (1725; reprint, Hildesheim: Verlag, 1971).

3. Balthasar Gibert, *Observations adressées à M. Rollin . . . , Ancien recteur et professeur royal, sur son Traité de la manière d'enseig-*

ner et d'étudier les belles lettres (Paris: François-Guillaume L'Hermite, 1727).

4. Gibert, *Jugemens*, 350–60.

5. Gibert, *Règles de l'éloquence,* 104.

6. Hugh Blair, *Lectures on Rhetoric and Belles Lettres,* ed. Harold F. Harding, 2 vols. (Carbondale: Southern Illinois University Press, 1965), 2:181–82.

7. Michel Le Guern, "La Méthode dans *La Rhétorique ou l'art de parler* de Bernard Lamy," in *Grammaire et méthode au XVIIe siècle,* ed. Pierre Swiggers (Leuven: Peeters, 1984), 49–67.

8. John T. Harwood, "Introduction," in *The Rhetorics of Thomas Hobbes and Bernard Lamy* (Carbondale: Southern Illinois University Press, 1986), 131. See also Le Guern, 50.

9. *Encyclopédie, ou Dictionnaire raisonné des sciences, des arts et des métiers,* s.v. "Rhétorique."

10. Thomas M. Carr, Jr., *Descartes and the Resilience of Rhetoric* (Carbondale: Southern Illinois University Press, 1990), 128.

11. René Descartes, *Discours de la Méthode,* ed. André Robinet (Paris: Larousse, 1972), 48.

12. Le Guern, 49–67; Carr, 134–35.

13. Another French rhetoric that combined rhetoric with poetic and other discursive genres was that of René Rapin. Rapin's work was neoclassical rather than modern, however. I have consulted it in translation as *The Whole Critical Works of Monr. Rapin,* trans. Basil Kennet, Mr. Rymer, and others, 2 vols. (London: Walthoe, 1731). Wilbur Samuel Howell (*Eighteenth-Century British Logic and Rhetoric* [Princeton: Princeton University Press, 1971], 520–25) has described Rapin's works and reported that his writings were initially collected and published in 1684.

14. Preface to *La Rhétorique ou l'art de parler,* 4th ed. (Amsterdam: Marrey, 1699), n.p. Translation in Harwood, 178. Generally, I have used the anonymous 1676 translation in Harwood when citing the work's first edition and provided my own translation for later editions that have not been translated. Also, since the later editions of *L'Art de parler* were substantially expanded, I have consulted the first (1676) edition, as well as a 1699 edition. As Carr has reported (pp. 128 and 193), Lamy's most substantial revision occurred in 1688; any edition produced after that date will include most of Lamy's significant additions to the work.

15. Preface to *L'Art de parler* (1699 ed.), n.p. My translation.

16. Preface to *L'Art de parler* (1699 ed.), n.p. My translation.

17. René Descartes, *Les Passions de l'âme* (Paris: Gallimard, 1988).

18. Descartes, *Passions,* 147.

19. *L'Art de parler* (Paris: Pralard, 1676), 193. Harwood edition, 292.

20. Jean-Paul Sermain, *Rhétorique et roman au dix-huitième siècle* (Oxford: Alden Press, 1985), 18. My translation.

21. Or, as James L. Golden and Edward P. J. Corbett put it, "By eliminating the role of discovery from *inventio,* Campbell, Blair, and Whately altered the starting point to be used in speech preparation. Speakers can assume that since arguments and proof are present from the outset, their principal challenge is to learn how to manage rather than invent or discover ideas." See *The Rhetoric of Blair, Campbell, and Whately* (New York: Holt, 1968), 14. See also Douglas W. Ehninger, "George Campbell and the Revolution in Inventional Theory," *Southern Speech Journal,* 15 (1950): 270–76.

22. *L'Art de parler* (1699 ed.), 304–5. Harwood edition, 343.

23. In his "Rules for the Direction of the Mind" (*Descartes Selections,* ed. Ralph M. Eaton [New York: Scribner's, 1977]), 40–41, Descartes stipulated that "Only those objects should engage our attention, to the sure and indubitable knowledge of which our mental powers seem to be adequate," and he supported this by saying that "there is scarce any question occurring in the sciences about which talented men have not disagreed. But whenever two men come to opposite decisions about the same matter one of them at least must certainly be in the wrong, and apparently there is not even one of them in the right; for if the reasoning of the second was sound and clear he would be able so to lay it before the other as finally to succeed in convincing *his* understanding also. Hence apparently we cannot attain to a perfect knowledge in any such case of probable opinion."

24. *L'Art de parler* (1699 ed.) 328. My translation.

25. [Antoine Arnauld and Pierre Nicole], *Logic, or the Art of Thinking,* trans. Thomas Spenser Baynes (Edinburgh: Sutherland & Knox, 1850), 175–228.

26. *L'Art de parler* (1676 ed.) 23–24. Harwood edition, 192–93.

27. Cicero, *Pro T. Annio Milone, etc.,* trans. N. H. Watts (Cambridge: Harvard University Press, 1958).

28. *L'Art de parler* (1676 ed.), 280. Harwood edition, 344.

29. *L'Art de parler* (1676 ed.), 330–31. Harwood edition, 374.

30. *L'Art de parler* (1699 ed.), 314–15. Harwood edition, 349–50.

31. Aristotle, *Topica,* trans. E. S. Forster (Cambridge: Harvard University Press, 1960).

32. Cicero, *De Inventione, De Optimo Genere Oratorum, Topica,* trans. H. M. Hubbell (Cambridge: Harvard University Press, 1960).

33. *L'Art de parler* (1699 ed.), 314–16; Arnauld and Nicole, *Logic,* 231–36.

34. *L'Art de parler* (1699 ed.), 308. Harwood edition, 345.

35. *L'Art de parler* (1699 ed.), 308. Harwood edition, 345.

36. François de Fénelon, *Dialogues sur l'éloquence* (Paris, Garnier Frères, 1866), 28; Wilbur Samuel Howell, trans., *Fénelon's Dialogues on Eloquence,* (Princeton: Princeton University Press, 1951), 85.

37. *L'Art de parler* (1676 ed.), 181–85. Harwood edition, 346–47.

38. *L'Art de parler* (1699 ed.), 315. Harwood edition, 350.

39. *L'Art de parler* (1699 ed.), 335. My translation.

40. *L'Art de parler* (1676 ed.), 302. Harwood edition, 357.

41. *L'Art de parler* (1699 ed.), 336.

42. *L'Art de parler* (1699 ed.), 329.

43. *L'Art de parler* (1699 ed.), 330. Harwood edition, 352.

44. *L'Art de parler* (1676 ed.), 74. My translation.

45. *L'Art de parler* (1676 ed.), 248–49. My translation.

46. *L'Art de parler* (1676 ed.), 209. Harwood edition, 304.

47. *L'Art de parler* (1676 ed.), 256. Harwood edition, 331.

48. *L'Art de parler* (Harwood edition), 221.

49. *L'Art de parler* (1676 ed.), 224. Harwood edition, 312.

50. *L'Art de parler* (1676 ed.), 253. My translation.

51. See Barbara Warnick, "The Old Rhetoric vs. the New Rhetoric: the Quarrel between the Ancients and the Moderns," *Communication Monographs* 49 (1982), 263–76.

52. French rhetoricians explicitly cited by the Scottish belletrists included Fénelon, Rollin, Crévier, and Gibert. These citation patterns are discussed in my introduction and chapter 2. Lamy's work was not cited by Smith, Blair, or Campbell.

53. Jean-Baptiste Dubos, *Réflexions critiques sur la poésie et sur la peinture* (Utrecht: E. Neaulme, 1732–36), 2:179.

54. Francis Hutcheson, *An Inquiry into the Original of our Ideas of Beauty and Virtue,* 4th ed. (London: Midwinter, 1738; Reprint, Westmead: Gregg, 1969), 80.

55. Charles Rollin, *De la Manière d'enseigner et d'étudier les Belles Lettres* (Lyon: Rusand, 1819), 2:203.

56. Fénelon, *Dialogues,* 35; Howell translation, 92–93.

57. Fénelon, *Dialogues,* 35; Howell translation, 93–94.

58. Wilbur Samuel Howell, *Poetics, Rhetoric, and Logic* (Ithaca, NY: Cornell University Press, 1975), 136.

59. Dubos, 1:15–16.

60. Dubos, 1:15.

61. Barbara Warnick, "Fénelon's Recommendations to the French

Academy Concerning Rhetoric," *Communication Monographs* 45 (1978), 75–78.

62. Dubos, 1:141.
63. Dubos, 1:129.
64. Dominique Bouhours, *La Manière de bien penser dans les ouvrages d'esprit* (1715; Reprint, Brighton: University of Sussex, 1971), 77.
65. François Fénelon, *Lettre à l'Académie,* ed. Ernesta Caldarini (Geneva: Librairie Droz, 1970), 42.
66. Fénelon, *Lettre,* 50. Translation from Barbara Warnick, ed. and trans., *Fénelon's Letter to the French Academy* (Lanham, MD: University Press of America, 1984), 66.
67. Fénelon, *Dialogues,* 59; Howell translation, 119–20.
68. Rollin, 2:201.
69. Bouhours, 100.
70. Fénelon, *Lettre,* 111. My translation, 95.
71. Dubos, 1:69.
72. Dubos, 1:44.
73. Dubos, 1:80.
74. Arnauld and Nicole, *Logic,* 65–72.
75. *L'Art de parler* (1676 ed.), 30. My translation.
76. Bouhours, 12.
77. Bouhours, 536; see also Rollin, 2:324–25.
78. Fénelon, *Lettre,* 72. My translation, 75.
79. Fénelon, *Lettre,* 71. My translation, 75.
80. Bouhours, 514.
81. Bouhours, 518.
82. Rollin, 2:57–58.

Chapter 2: Propriety

1. Robert Garapon, "Sur le sens du mot «raison» au dix-septième siècle," in *Convergences: Rhetoric and Poetic in Seventeenth-Century France,* ed. David Lee Rubin and Mary B. McKinley (Columbus: Ohio State University Press, 1989), 34–44.
2. References to the French editions of these two works will be to *Dialogues sur l'éloquence* (Paris: Garnier Frères, 1866) and to *Lettre à l'Académie,* ed. Ernesta Caldarini (Geneva: Librairie Droz, 1970). English translations cited are Wilbur Samuel Howell, trans., *Fénelon's Dialogues on Eloquence* (Princeton: Princeton University Press, 1951) and Barbara Warnick, ed. and trans., *Fénelon's Letter to the French Academy* (Lanham, MD: University Press of America, 1984). The probable composition date of the

Dialogues is 1679; the *Lettre* was written in 1713 and first published in 1716. The *Dialogues* were not published until 1718. See Caldarini (11–13) for a publication history of these works in the eighteenth century.

3. François Varillon, *Fénelon et le pur amour* (Paris: Editions du Seuil, 1957), 79. My translation of Varillon's phrase, "une nostalgie désesperée de l'unité."

4. Christoph Strosetzki, *Rhétorique de la conversation,* trans. Sabine Seubert (Paris: Papers on Seventeenth-Century Literature, 1984), 1–84.

5. *Le Grand Robert de la langue française,* 2nd ed., s.v. "bienséance." My translation.

6. Strosetzki, 119. See also Rémy G. Saisselin, *The Rule of Reason and the Ruses of the Heart* (Cleveland, OH: Case Western Reserve University, 1970), 48–49.

7. Jean Mesnard, "Vraie et fausse beauté dans l'esthétique au dix-septième siècle," in *Convergences,* 13. My translation.

8. Boileau-Despréaux, *Art poétique,* Chant III in *Oeuvres complètes* (Gallimard, 1966), 170. "What is true sometimes does not seem true;" or "Truth sometimes lacks verisimilitude."

9. Aaron Kibédi Varga, "La Vraisemblance—Problèmes de terminologie, problèmes de poétique," in *Critique et création littéraires en France au XVIIe siècle* (Paris: Centre National de la Recherche Scientifique, 1977), 328. My translation.

10. Saisselin, 208.

11. Elbert B. O. Borgerhoff, *The Freedom of French Classicism* (Princeton: Princeton University Press, 1950), 224.

12. Fénelon, *Lettre,* 144; my translation, 111 ("Tout est plein de fenêtres, de roses, et de pointes.")

13. In her substantial study of the Fénelonian aesthetic, Jeanne-Lydie Goré insisted that "Poussin incarne l'idéal esthétique de Fénelon" (*L'Itinéraire de Fénelon: Humanisme et spiritualité* [Paris: Presses Universitaires de France, 1957], 601). And, as Jacques Thullier has noted, the "nature" depicted in Poussin's work is reformed and artificial: "Qu'est-ce qu'un tableau de Poussin? On se tromperait en louant la vérité de la représentation. L'univers de Poussin est systématiquement artificiel. . . . Et à mesure qu'évolue l'art de Poussin, il n'hésite pas à aligner ses personnages en manière de bas-relief, ou à les installer en groupes symétriques réglés par un metteur en scène trop ostensiblement présent." ("La Notion d'imitation dans la pensée artistique du XVIIe siècle," in *Critique et création littéraires,* 368.) There seems to be some incompatibility, then, between the art-

less nature Fénelon often defended and his own aesthetic preferences.

14. Goré, 672. My translation.
15. Fénelon, *Dialogues,* 8. Howell translation, 64.
16. [Longinus] *On the Sublime* 2.25–27.
17. Fénelon, *Lettre.* My translation, 67–68.
18. Wilbur Samuel Howell, "Oratory and Poetry in Fénelon's Literary Theory," in *Poetics, Rhetoric, and Logic* (Ithaca, NY: Cornell University Press, 1975), 134.
19. Fénelon, *Dialogues,* 35–36. Howell translation, 92–94.
20. Howell, "Oratory and Poetry," 138.
21. Fénelon, *Lettre,* 50. My translation, 66.
22. Fénelon, *Lettre,* 51. My translation, 66.
23. Fénelon, *Dialogues,* 31. Howell translation, 89.
24. Fénelon, *Lettre,* 50. My translation, 66.
25. Fénelon, *Dialogues,* 51. Howell translation, 111.
26. Fénelon, *Dialogues,* 53. Howell translation, 114.
27. Fénelon, *Dialogues,* 5. Howell translation, 61.
28. Fénelon, *Dialogues,* 51–52. Howell translation, 112–13.
29. Fénelon, *Dialogues,* 39. Howell translation, 99.
30. Fénelon, *Dialogues,* 40–41. Howell translation, 100.
31. Fénelon, *Dialogues,* 4–5. Howell translation, 60–61; and Fénelon, *Lettre,* 90–93. My translation, 86–87.
32. Fénelon, *Lettre,* 75. My translation, 77.
33. Adam Smith, *Lectures on Rhetoric and Belles Lettres,* ed. John M. Lothian (London: Nelson, 1963). On the dubious quality of this manuscript, see my introduction, n. 50. See also n. 36, this chapter.
34. See Dugold Stewart's "Account of the Life and Writings of Adam Smith, LL.D." in Smith's *Essays on Philosophical Subjects* (1795; Reprint, Hildesheim: Verlag, 1982), lxxxvii: "A few days before his death, finding his end approaching rapidly, he gave orders to destroy all his manuscripts . . . and they were accordingly committed to the flames. . . . There can be no doubt that they consisted, in part, of the lectures on rhetoric, which he read at Edinburgh in the year 1748. . . ." Stewart reported that Smith had long planned to destroy his papers before he died. Certainly, the appearance of Blair's *Lectures on Rhetoric and Belles Lettres* in 1783 offered Smith little incentive after that time to revise his own lectures for publication.
35. Like his Scottish colleagues, George Campbell and Hugh Blair, Smith read many French authors in the original language. Lothian (xiv) reported in his "Introduction" to Smith's *Lectures* that

"Smith had always been in the habit of studying French authors, and of translating passages from their works in order to improve his own style. . . ." Decipherable references to French authors in the Lothian edition identify Dubos (72), La Bruyère (76), Descartes (140), and a dozen others as sources.

36. Adam Smith, *Lectures on Rhetoric and Belles Lettres,* ed. J. C. Bryce (Oxford: Clarendon, 1983), 6. All subsequent references to this work will be to this edition.
37. Smith, *Lectures,* 25.
38. Adam Smith, *The Theory of Moral Sentiments,* ed. D. D. Raphael and A. L. Macfie (Oxford; Clarendon, 1976), 9.
39. Smith, *Theory,* 18.
40. Smith, *Lectures,* 40.
41. Smith, *Lectures,* 42–109.
42. Bryce, "Introduction" to Smith's *Lectures,* 12–13.
43. Smith, *Lectures,* 148.
44. Smith, *Lectures,* 42.
45. Smith, *Lectures,* 25–26.
46. Smith, *Lectures,* 22.
47. Smith, *Lectures,* 116.
48. Smith, *Lectures,* 23.
49. Smith, *Lectures,* 40.
50. Smith, *Lectures,* 111.
51. Smith, *Lectures,* 147.
52. Smith, *Lectures,* 159.
53. Smith, *Lectures,* 98.
54. Smith, *Essays,* 154.
55. George Campbell, *Lectures on Pulpit Eloquence* (London: John Bumpus, 1824), 175.
56. George Campbell, *The Philosophy of Rhetoric* (New York: Harper & Brothers, 1859); Dubos, 136, 155; Bouhours, 301, 376, 420; Rollin, 28, 368; and Boileau, 302.
57. On impoverishment of the French language, see George Campbell, *The Philosophy of Rhetoric,* ed. Lloyd F. Bitzer (Carbondale: Southern Illinois University Press, 1963; Revised 1988), 398–99; and Warnick, *Fénelon's Letter,* 56–57. Subsequent references to Campbell's *Philosophy* will be to Bitzer's edition. On the superiority of Greek and Latin for capturing meter, see Campbell, *Philosophy,* 321 and Warnick, *Fénelon's Letter,* 73; on borrowing and adapting words, see Campbell, *Philosophy,* 176, 298 and Warnick, *Fénelon's Letter,* 57–59.
58. In the same editions cited in n. 57, see Campbell, 180, 313, 218 and in Warnick, *Fénelon's Letter,* see 66, 69, 68, 67. On organization, see also the passages cited in nn. 25–27 of this chapter.

59. On p. 216 of *The Philosophy of Rhetoric,* he also lists elegance, animation, and music as original qualities of style but he does not discuss them at any length.

60. On vivacity, see Lloyd F. Bitzer, "Hume's Philosophy in George Campbell's *Philosophy of Rhetoric,*" *Philosophy and Rhetoric,* 2 (1969), 139–66.

61. Campbell, *Philosophy,* 215.

62. Campbell, *Philosophy,* 190.

63. Campbell, *Philosophy,* 145.

64. Campbell, *Lectures,* 191.

65. Campbell, *Lectures,* 193, 209.

66. Anand C. Chitnis, *The Scottish Enlightenment: A Social History* (London: Croon Helm, 1976), 16–20.

67. Home to [Lord] Milton, August, 1756, NLS 16696: 74; as cited in Richard B. Sher, *Church and University in the Scottish Enlightenment* (Edinburgh: Edinburgh University Press, 1985), 108.

68. Chitnis, 111.

69. Campbell, *Lectures,* 181.

70. Campbell, *Philosophy,* 83.

71. Hugh Blair, *Lectures on Rhetoric and Belles Lettres,* ed. Harold F. Harding, 2 vols. (Carbondale: Southern Illinois University Press, 1965), 1:381. In his "Introduction", Harding noted that Blair actually attended Smith's lectures in 1748 and perused Smith's notes before beginning his own course in 1759. Blair's lectures were first published in 1783. Harding argued (pp. xxii–xxv) that charges that Blair plagiarized from Smith were unwarranted. See also n. 34.

72. Blair, *Lectures,* 1:154–55, 182, 209; 2:104.

73. Blair, *Lectures,* 2:33–34.

74. Blair, *Lectures,* 2:33, 170, 242, 248.

75. Blair, *Lectures,* 1:33 on Demosthenes; 1:262 and 2:21 on unobtrusiveness; 1:55, 165 on suitable style; and 1:46 on the sublime.

76. Blair, *Lectures,* 1:368.

77. Blair, *Lectures,* 1:189.

78. Blair's taxonomy of the "characters of style" also included dry, plain, neat, elegant, flowery, simple, affected, and vehement; see his *Lectures,* 1:363–400.

79. Blair's theory of style appears to have been one of his few original contributions to rhetorical theory. See my article, "The Most Significant Passage in Hugh Blair's *Lectures on Rhetoric and Belles Lettres,*" *Rhetoric Society Quarterly* 17 (1987), 301–04.

80. Blair, *Lectures,* 1:187.

81. Campbell, *Philosophy,* 190–204; Blair, *Lectures,* 1:187–88.

82. Hugh Blair, "A Critical Dissertation on the Poems of Ossian," in *The Poems of Ossian,* trans. James Macpherson, Esq. (Leipzig: Bernhard Tauchnitz, 1847), 111.
83. Blair, *Lectures,* 2:58.
84. Blair, *Lectures,* 1:390.
85. Blair, *Lectures,* 1:279 and 2:167.
86. Blair, *Lectures,* 2:108.
87. Blair, *Lectures,* 2:56–57.

Chapter 3: The Sublime

1. As Wilbur Samuel Howell put it: ". . . Fénelon began rhetoric anew, not by repudiating ancient doctrine, but by objecting to the rigid routines which Ramus had derived from the ancients, and by going on from there to select from ancient doctrine those insights which had never lost their modernity." Howell then noted Fénelon's disparagement of the commonplaces and praised his fusion of aesthetic standards with other elements of a modern theory. See Howell's "Introduction" to his translation of the *Dialogues on Eloquence* (Princeton: Princeton University Press, 1951), 45. On the Academy's reception of Fénelon's *Lettre,* see Gottfried Landolf, *Esthétique de Fénelon* (Zurich: Leeman, 1914), 89–90.
2. Ernst Cassirer, *The Philosophy of the Enlightenment,* trans. Fritz C. A. Koelin and James P. Pettegrove (Princeton: Princeton University Press, 1951), 278–304.
3. Cassirer, 279.
4. Nicolas Boileau–Despréaux, *Oeuvres complètes,* ed. Antoine Adam (Paris: Editions Gallimard, 1966), 157–85.
5. Jeanne Haight, *The Concept of Reason in French Classical Literature, 1635–1690* (Toronto: University of Toronto Press, 1982).
6. Cassirer, 294.
7. Dominique Bouhours, *La Manière de bien penser dans les ouvrages d'esprit* (1715; Reprint, Brighton: University of Sussex, 1971).
8. Cassirer, 301.
9. Jean-Baptiste Dubos, *Réflexions critiques sur la poésie et sur la peinture,* 3 vols. (Utrecht: E. Naulme, 1732–36). Dubos' work will be discussed at length in chapter 4. Since his aesthetics was avowedly subjectivist and empirical, it fit in well with the account Cassirer constructed of the shift from rationalism to empiricism.
10. Cassirer, 303.
11. Boileau, *Oeuvres complètes,* 333–440. All citations from this

work and its preface will be from this edition as cited in n. 4 and will be my translations from the French. This edition is for the most part a reproduction of the 1701 edition of Boileau's *Oeuvres diverses*. The spelling and diacritical marks, while not correct by contemporary standards, have all been reproduced exactly. *On the Sublime* was for a long time thought to have been written by Longinus of Palmyra in the third century A.D. The treatise has since been shown to date from the first, not the third, century and to be the work of an anonymous author. (See the Introduction to W. Rhys Roberts' translation of *On the Sublime* [Cambridge: The University Press, 1899], 1–23). After noting the mistaken authorship, most scholars writing on the topic still refer to the treatise as Longinus' for convenience. I shall follow this convention. In *The Sublime: A Study of Critical Theories of the Eighteenth Century in England* (Ann Arbor: University of Michigan Press, 1960), 29, Samuel H. Monk noted the apparent irony of the simultaneous publication of these two works: "Boileau's *L'Art poétique* is a complete expression of the neo-classic code. As such it became one of the chief documents of the literary tories of the eighteenth century; as such it was one of the chief rationalizations of a type of art that the nineteenth century regarded as anathema. The translation of Longinus, taking quite a different course, was, throughout the neo-classic period in England, the center around which revolved many of the ideas that influenced poets to lay the old aside. Thus Boileau unwittingly set at work in the world two forces that eventually became mutually hostile. Viewed historically, his credo has the dual physiognomy of Janus."

12. For an account of Boileau's controversy with the moderns, see Barbara Warnick, "The Old Rhetoric vs. the New Rhetoric: the Quarrel between the Ancients and the Moderns," *Communication Monographs* 49 (1982), 263–76.

13. Boileau, 548–49.

14. See Antoine Adam, *Histoire de la littérature française au XVIIe siècle* (Paris: Domat, 1956), 5:77: "Lui qui longtemps avait professé le cartesianism, il comprenait maintenant que la nouvelle philosophie mettait en question toute poésie."

15. Jules Brody, "Boileau and Longinus" (Ph.D. diss., Columbia University, 1956), 192.

16. Boileau, 338.

17. Boileau, 348.

18. Brody, 64.

19. Julian Eugene White, Jr., *Nicolas Boileau* (New York: Twayne Publishers, 1969), 161.

20. W. Hamilton Fyfe's Introduction to his translation of [Longinus] *On the Sublime* (Cambridge: Harvard University Press, 1927), xviii.
21. Brody, 21–22.
22. François de Fénelon, *Lettre à l'Académie,* ed. Ernesta Caldarini (Genève: Librairie Droz, 1970), 58, 133–34, 135.
23. Charles Rollin, *De la Manière d'enseigner et d'étudier les Belles Lettres,* 4 vols. (Lyon: Rusand, 1819), 2:69, 70, 72; on Lamy, see Brody, 22.
24. John Holmes, *The Art of Rhetoric Made Easy or, the Elements of Oratory,* 2nd ed., 2 vols. (London: Hitch & Hawes, 1755); Edmund Burke, *A Philosophical Enquiry into the Origin of our Ideas of the Sublime and Beautiful,* ed. James T. Boulton (London: Routledge, 1958); John Lawson, *Lectures concerning Oratory,* ed. E. Neal Claussen and Karl R. Wallace (1758; Reprint, Carbondale: Southern Illinois University Press, 1972), 67–78 and 326–27; Henry Home (Lord Kames), *Elements of Criticism,* 3 vols. (1762; Reprint, New York: Johnson Reprint Collection, 1967), 1:277–302; and Adam Smith, *Lectures on Rhetoric and Belles Lettres,* ed. J. C. Bryce (Oxford: Clarendon, 1983), 190–95.
25. Brody, 14.
26. E. Egger, *L'Hellénisme en France* (Paris: Didier, 1869).
27. Alexander F. B. Clark, *Boileau and the French Classical Critics in England* (Paris: Edouard Champion, 1925), 362.
28. Brody, 58–182.
29. Boileau, 337.
30. [Longinus] *On the Sublime* 8.12–25.
31. Dissociation disengages a notion or the use of a term from associations normally identified with it. Dissociation resolves incompatibilities and reforms traditional conceptions. It sets up a hierarchy between two terms—a Term I viewed as only apparent, and a Term II viewed as "real." See Chaim Perelman and Lucie Olbrechts-Tyteca, *The New Rhetoric: A Treatise on Argumentation,* trans. John Wilkinson and Purcell Weaver (Notre Dame: University of Notre Dame Press, 1969), 438–41. In the remainder of this chapter "the Sublime" in this Term II sense will be capitalized to distinguish it from the general sublime style.
32. Boileau, 338.
33. Boileau, 341. *On the Sublime* 1.9–12.
34. Brody, 174.
35. Boileau, 551.
36. For examples, see Boileau, 342, 348, 395.
37. Gordon Pocock, *Boileau and the Nature of Neo-Classicism* (Cambridge: Cambridge University Press, 1980), 10.

38. Boileau, 374. *On the Sublime* 22.25–28.
39. Boileau, 338.
40. Boileau, 551–52.
41. White, 158.
42. Although Howell (p. 131) speculates that Holmes may have used English translations by Pulteney, Welsted, or an anonymous translator, all drawn wholly or partly from Boileau's French, my examination of Holmes' work indicates that there is little or no correlation between Boileau's version and Holmes' product. Certainly, Boileau popularized *On the Sublime* in England and Holmes was aware of Boileau's commentary, but he does not appear to have relied on any prior translative work based on Boileau. See Holmes, *The Art of Rhetoric,* 2:6, 12, 21, 61.
43. See Walter John Hipple, *The Beautiful, the Sublime, and the Picturesque* (Carbondale: Southern Illinois University Press, 1957), 13–36.
44. Joseph Priestley, *A Course of Lectures on Oratory and Criticism,* ed. Vincent M. Bevilacqua and Richard Murphy (Carbondale: Southern Illinois University Press, 1965).
45. Preface to Priestley's *Lectures,* i–ii.
46. Bevilacqua and Murphy's Introduction, xxiii–xxiv.
47. Priestley, 151.
48. Priestley, 84, 98, and 101.
49. Priestley, 158.
50. Priestley, 154.
51. Priestley, 157.
52. Priestley, 244.
53. George Campbell, *The Philosophy of Rhetoric,* ed. Lloyd F. Bitzer (Carbondale: Southern Illinois University Press, 1963; Revised, 1988), lxxiv–lxxv.
54. Campbell, 1.
55. Campbell, 1.
56. Campbell, 3.
57. Fénelon, *Lettre à l'Académie,* 88. My translation.
58. Recall that for Descartes and Lamy (chapter 1), admiration was not only *a* passion; it was the *chief* passion. See René Descartes, *Les Passions de l'âme* (Paris: Gallimard, 1988), 190.
59. Campbell, 3.
60. Campbell, 6.
61. Bouhours is cited on 279, 357; Buffier on 38, 42, 234; Dubos on 113, 129; Rollin on 6, 349; and Boileau on 280.
62. Campbell published in 1789 an English translation from the Greek of the new Testament Gospels; he also included citations

from Greek in his *Philosophy of Rhetoric*. See, for example, 28, 72, 93, 137, and 164.

63. Hugh Blair, *Lectures on Rhetoric and Belles Lettres*, ed. Harold F. Harding, 2 vols. (Carbondale: Southern Illinois University Press, 1965), 1:xi.

64. Patricia Bizzell and Bruce Herzberg, *The Rhetorical Tradition* (Boston: St. Martin's, 1990), 656.

65. In his *Eighteenth-Century British Logic and Rhetoric* (Princeton: Princeton University Press, 1971), Howell questioned the merit of Blair's *Lectures* (648) and criticized their lack of depth and penetration (655).

66. Hipple, 122.

67. Douglas W. Ehninger and James Golden, "The Intrinsic Sources of Blair's Popularity," *Southern Speech Journal* 21 (1955), 12–30.

68. Richard B. Sher, *Church and University in the Scottish Enlightenment* (Edinburgh: Edinburgh University Press, 1985), 29.

69. Blair's Preface, iv.

70. Blair's Preface, iv.

71. Fénelon 2:34, 170, 242, 248; Dubos 1:252, 2:248; Fontenelle 2:237, 248, 296. Boileau is explicitly cited in 1:76 and 2:248, 249, 370, although Blair used Boileau's ideas more frequently than he cited him. The index, which accompanied the reprinted edition, is quite unreliable.

72. Blair 1:46.

73. Blair 2:54.

74. Blair 1:59.

75. Blair 1:58.

76. Blair 1:76.

77. Blair 1:76.

78. Blair 1:75.

79. Blair 1:70.

Chapter 4: Taste

1. Rémy G. Saisselin, *Taste in Eighteenth Century France* (Syracuse, NY: Syracuse University Press, 1965), 52.

2. Charles Rollin, *De la Manière d'enseigner et d'étudier les Belles Lettres,* 4 vols. (Lyon: Rusand, 1819), 1:162. My translation.

3. Hugh Blair, *Lectures on Rhetoric and Belles Lettres,* ed. Harold F. Harding, 2 vols. (Carbondale: Southern Illinois University Press, 1965), 1:9.

4. Blair, 1:10.

5. Walter J. Hipple, Jr., "Introduction," in Alexander Gerard, *An Essay on Taste,* 3rd ed. (1780; Reprint, Gainesville, FL: Scholars' Facsimiles and Reprints, 1963), xi.

6. Work of Adam Smith relevant to aesthetics will not be treated in this chapter because Smith's lectures on rhetoric seem to have been originally composed prior to the appearance of most eighteenth-century writings on taste. In any case, the student copyists' notes that we possess do not treat the topic of taste to any significant extent. For Smith's thinking on the fine arts, see his "Of the Imitative Arts" in *Essays on Philosophical Subjects* (1795; Reprint, Hildesheim: Verlag, 1982), 133–84.

7. George Campbell, *The Philosophy of Rhetoric,* ed. Lloyd F. Bitzer (Carbondale: Southern Illinois University Press, 1963; Revised, 1988), 1–2.

8. In Dugald Stewart's biography of Thomas Reid (Reid's *Works,* ed. William Hamilton, 8th ed., 2 vols. [Edinburgh: Thin, 1895], 1:6–8) one finds an extensive account of mutual acquaintance and respect among these men. Reid was a member, along with Campbell and James Beattie, of the Aberdeen Philosophical Society formed in 1758 which spent much of its time debating Hume's theories. Stewart also reported that Reid, wishing to avoid misrepresentation of Hume's views, sought to submit his reasonings to Hume's private examination. "With this in view, he [Reid] availed himself of the good offices of Dr. Blair, with whom both he and Hume had long lived in habits of friendship." (p. 7) Hume and Blair were also founding members of the Select Society of Edinburgh. See Roger L. Emerson, "The Social Composition of Enlightened Scotland: the Select Society of Edinburgh, 1754–1764," *Studies on Voltaire and the Eighteenth Century* 114 (1973), 291–329. Reid, Campbell, and Blair were all ministers of the Presbyterian church and active in church governance. See also Anand C. Chitnis, *The Scottish Enlightenment* (London: Croon Helm, 1976), 199–202; and Richard Sher, *Church and University in the Scottish Enlightenment* (Edinburgh: Edinburgh University Press, 1985).

9. David Hume, *Essays: Moral, Political, and Literary,* ed. Eugene F. Miller (Indianapolis, IN: Liberty Classics, 1984), 226–49. See also Noel Carroll, "Hume's Standard of Taste," *Journal of Aesthetics and Art Criticism* 43 (1984), 181–94; and Jeffrey Weiand, "Hume's Two Standards of Taste," *The Philosophical Quarterly* 34 (1984), 129–42.

10. Hipple's Introduction to Gerard, vi.

11. Hipple's Introduction to Gerard, xv.

12. Other essays by Hume relating to aesthetics include "Of the Delicacy of Taste and Passion," "Of the Rise and Progress of the Arts and Sciences," and "Of Refinement in the Arts." (These are all included in the volume of essays cited in n. 9, *Essays.*)

13. *The Encyclopedia of Philosophy,* s. v. "Hume, David."
14. Hume, 231. My emphasis.
15. Hume, 241.
16. Hume, 233–34.
17. Hume, 232.
18. Hume, 235.
19. Hume, 234–35. The passage is taken from *Don Quixote,* pt. 2, chap. 13.
20. Hume, 237.
21. Hume, 237.
22. Hume, 238.
23. Hume, 239.
24. Hume, 240. My emphasis.
25. Hume, 237.
26. Hume, 241.
27. Hume, 242.
28. Gerard, 227.
29. Gerard, 232.
30. Gerard, 235.
31. Gerard, 235.
32. Gerard, 238.
33. Hipple's Introduction to Gerard, vii.
34. Gerard, 8.
35. Gerard, 9.
36. Gerard, 12.
37. Gerard, 29.
38. Gerard, 55.
39. Marjorie Grene, "Gerard's *Essay on Taste,*" *Modern Philology* 41 (1943), 45.
40. Gerard, 144–45.
41. Gerard, 145–46.
42. Gerard, 148.
43. Gerard, 88.
44. Vincent Bevilacqua, "Campbell, Priestley, and the Controversy concerning Common Sense," *Southern Speech Journal* 30 (1964), 87.
45. See Dugald Stewart, *The Collected Works,* ed. William Hamilton, 8 vols. (Edinburgh: Constable, 1855), 5:189–406; and James R. Irvine, "James Beattie's Psychology of Taste," *Western Speech Journal* 34 (1970), 21–28.
46. Stewart's "Account of the Life and Writings of Thomas Reid, D.D." in Reid's *Works,* 1:28.
47. Reid, 1:421.

48. Reid, 1:455.
49. Reid, 1:457.
50. Stewart's account of Reid, 1:27.
51. Stewart's account of Reid, 1:27.
52. Reid, 1:490.
53. Reid, 1:491.
54. Reid, 1:493.
55. Reid, 1:494.
56. Reid, 1:453.
57. Reid, 1:452–53.
58. Reid, 1:453.
59. Reid, 1:492.
60. Reid, 1:492.
61. Reid, 1:492.
62. Reid, 1:419.
63. David O. Robbins, "The Aesthetics of Thomas Reid," *Journal of Aesthetics and Art Criticism* 1 (1942): 40; on Reid's aesthetics, see also Martin Kallich, "The Argument against the Association of Ideas in Eighteenth-Century Aesthetics," *Modern Language Quarterly* 15 (1954): 125–36; and Keith Lehrer, "Beyond Impressions and Ideas: Hume vs. Reid," in *The "Science of Man" in the Scottish Enlightenment,* ed. Peter Jones (Edinburgh: Edinburgh University Press, 1989), 108–23.
64. Blair, 1:17 cited Jean d'Alembert's essay on taste, Jean Baptiste Dubos' *Réflexions critiques sur la poësie et sur la peinture,* Edmund Burke's *Philosophical Enquiry into the Origin of our Ideas of the Sublime and the Beautiful,* and Kames' essay on taste. Dubos' work is discussed in the last section of this chapter. See d'Alembert, *Oeuvres* (Paris: Belin, 1822) 4:326–33; Henry Home (Lord Kames) *Elements of Criticism,* 3 vols. (1762; Reprint, New York: Johnson Reprint Collection, 1967) 3:351–74; and Burke's *Philosophical Enquiry,* ed. James T. Boulton (London: Routledge & Kegan Paul, 1958).
65. Bevilacqua noted that Blair's lectures, begun in 1759, were not substantially changed between then and 1783 when they were published. See "Philosophical Assumptions underlying Hugh Blair's *Lectures on Rhetoric and Belles Lettres,*" *Western Speech Journal* 31 (1967): 150.
66. As noted in n. 64, Kames' *Elements of Criticism* appeared in 1762. On Blair's relationship with Kames, see Bevilacqua, "Lord Kames' Theory of Rhetoric," *Speech Monographs* 30 (1963): 324. Since Blair was transmitting Reid's writings to Hume (fn. 8), he probably read prepublication versions of Reid's views as well.

67. Kames, 3:355–56.
68. Kames, 3:364–65.
69. Kames, 3:356.
70. Kames, 3:369.
71. Blair, 1:30.
72. Blair, 1:17, 30.
73. Bevilacqua, "Philosophical Assumptions underlying Hugh Blair's *Lectures* . . .," 160–64; Harold F. Harding's Introduction to Blair's *Lectures,* 1:xxi, xxvi.
74. Blair, 1:32.
75. Blair, 1:16.
76. Blair, 1:16–7.
77. Blair, 1:19.
78. Blair, 1:24. Hume (p. 236) observed "A good palate is not tried by strong flavours; but by a mixture of small ingredients, where we are still sensible of each part, notwithstanding its minuteness and its confusion with the rest." Blair's only alteration to this passage was to make it more wordy.
79. Blair, 1:20.
80. Blair, 1:21; Hume, 237.
81. Blair, 1:32.
82. Francis Hutcheson, *An Inquiry into the Original of our Ideas of Beauty and Virtue,* 4th ed. (London: Midwinter, 1738; Reprint, Westmead: Gregg, 1969).
83. Hutcheson, 80.
84. Hutcheson, 29.
85. Hutcheson, 41.
86. Carolyn Korsmeyer, "The Two Beauties: A Perspective on Hutcheson's Aesthetics," *Journal of Aesthetics and Art Criticism* 38 (1979), 145. See also Michael Cardy, "Crousaz and Hutcheson: Two Contributors to Aesthetic Ideas in the Early Eighteenth Century," *Humanities Association Review* 31 (1980), 29–44; and Emily Michael, "Francis Hutcheson on Aesthetic Perception and Aesthetic Pleasure," *British Journal of Aesthetics* 24 (1984), 241–55.
87. Dabney Townsend, "From Shaftesbury to Kant: The Development of the Concept of Aesthetic Experience," *Journal of the History of Ideas* 48 (1987), 296.
88. Campbell, lxxi.
89. Campbell, lxxii–lxxiii. My emphasis.
90. Campbell, 81.
91. Campbell, 92.
92. Campbell, 94.

93. Campbell, 3.
94. Campbell, 37–38.
95. Campbell, 73.
96. Campbell, 74.
97. Campbell, 75.
98. Campbell, 119.
99. Of course, Gerard and Campbell, who held Humean views of how the mind worked, also had commonsense sympathies. For example, they took the principles of universal causation, uniformity of nature, existence of the external world, and credit to the testimony of others as convictions.
100. Hume, 240.
101. Gerard, 88.
102. Hume, 237.
103. Dubos, *Réflexions critiques sur la poësie et sur la peinture,* 3 vols. (Utrecht: E. Neaulme, 1732–36). All translations from Dubos in this chapter are mine.
104. T. M. Mustoxidi, *Histoire de l'esthétique française,* 1700–1900 (Paris: Champion, 1920), 17. My translation.
105. Saisselin, *The Rule of Reason and the Ruses of the Heart* (Cleveland, OH: Case Western Reserve, 1970), 263.
106. Jones, *Hume's Sentiments: Their Ciceronian and French Context* (Edinburgh: Edinburgh University Press, 1982), 106.
107. Gerard cited Dubos on pp. 81, 95, 106, 108–9, 135, 140, and 225 of his essay. He cited Bouhours five times and Boileau and Crousaz one time each.
108. Blair, 1:17, 253; 2:248.
109. Campbell, 119, 123.
110. Dubos, 2:8.
111. Dubos, 1:104.
112. Dubos, 2:178.
113. Jones, 115.
114. Dubos, 2:178.
115. Dubos, 2:179.
116. Jones, 98.
117. Dubos, 2:178.
118. Dubos, 2:3.
119. Dubos, 2:183–84.
120. Dubos, 2:182.
121. Dubos, 2:1.
122. Basil Munteano, "Les Prémisses rhétoriques du système de l'Abbé du Bos," *Rivista di Letterature Moderne e Comparate* 10 (1957), 11. My translation. See also his "L'Abbé du Bos: Esthé-

ticien de la persuasion passionnelle," *Revue de littérature comparée* 30 (1956), 318–49.

Conclusion

1. George Campbell, *The Philosophy of Rhetoric,* ed. Lloyd F. Bitzer (Carbondale: Southern Illinois University Press, 1963; Revised, 1988), 3.
2. J. T. Boulton's "Introduction" to Edmund Burke's *A Philosophical Enquiry into the Origin of our Ideas of the Sublime and Beautiful* (London: Routledge and Kegan Paul, 1958), xxviii.
3. I again want to emphasize that each French theorist discussed here is considered as "representative" of French belletristic thought *vis à vis* any given topic. Fénelon was of course not the only French theorist to consider propriety, nor was Dubos the only critic to write on taste. It would be fair to say, however, that the French theorists discussed in this book held views similar to the other theorists of their time and milieu. And, in fact, Fénelon's views on propriety, Boileau's on the Sublime, and Dubos' on taste were signal theories to which their successors looked for French thinking on these matters.
4. Lloyd Bitzer, who has edited Campbell's *The Philosophy of Rhetoric,* emphasized Hume's influence on Campbell. See his "Hume's Philosophy in George Campbell's *Philosophy of Rhetoric*" *Philosophy and Rhetoric* 2 (1969): 139–66 and the introduction to his edition of *The Philosophy of Rhetoric* (Carbondale: Southern Illinois University Press, 1963; Revised, 1988). Other critics, particularly Vincent Bevilacqua and Dennis R. Bormann, emphasize the commonsense influence on Campbell. The issue has not yet been satisfactorily resolved, in my opinion. See Bevilacqua's, "Campbell, Priestley, and the Controversy Concerning Common Sense," *Southern Speech Journal* 30 (1964): 79–98; and his "Philosophical Origins of George Campbell's *Philosophy of Rhetoric,*" *Speech Monographs* 32 (1965): 1–12. See also Bormann, "Some 'Common Sense' about Campbell, Hume, and Reid: The Extrinsic Evidence," *Quarterly Journal of Speech* 71 (1985): 395–421.
5. Campbell, 3.

Selected References

Aristotle. *The "Art" of Rhetoric.* Translated by John Henry Freese. Cambridge: Harvard University Press, 1975.

———. *Nicomachean Ethics.* Translated by Martin Ostwald. Indianapolis: Bobbs-Merrill, 1962.

Arnauld, Antoine, and Pierre Nicole. *The Art of Thinking.* Translated by James Dickoff and Patricia James. New York: Bobbs-Merrill, 1964.

———. *La Logique, ou l'art de penser.* 1683. Reprint. Edited by Pierre Clair and François Girbal. Paris: Presses Universitaires de France, 1965.

Atkinson, Geoffroy, and Abraham C. Keller. *Prelude to the Enlightenment 1690–1740.* Seattle, WA: University of Washington Press, 1970.

Bacon, Francis. *Advancement of Learning and Novum Organum.* New York: Collier, 1900.

Bailly, Auguste. *L'Ecole classique française: Les doctrines et les hommes.* Paris: Librairie Armand Colin, 1947.

Beardsley, Monroe C. *Aesthetics from Classical Greece to the Present: A Short History.* New York: Macmillan, 1966.

Bevilacqua, Vincent M. "The Rhetorical Theory of Henry Home, Lord Kames." Ph.D. diss., University of Illinois, 1961.

———. "Lord Kames's Theory of Rhetoric." *Speech Monographs* 30 (1963): 309–327.

———. "Campbell, Priestley, and the Controversy Concerning Common Sense." *Southern Speech Journal* 30 (1964): 79–98.

———. "Philosophical Origins of George Campbell's *Philosophy of Rhetoric*." *Speech Monographs* 32 (1965): 1–12.

———. "Philosophical Assumptions Underlying Hugh Blair's *Lectures on Rhetoric and Belles Lettres*." *Western Speech Journal* 31 (1967): 150–64.

Bitzer, Lloyd F. "Hume's Philosophy in George Campbell's *Philosophy of Rhetoric*." *Philosophy and Rhetoric* 2 (1969): 139–66.

Bizzell, Patricia, and Bruce Herzberg, eds. *The Rhetorical Tradition.* Boston: St. Martin's, 1990.

Blair, Hugh. *Lectures on Rhetoric and Belles Lettres.* London: J. F. Dove, 1914.

161

————. *Lectures on Rhetoric and Belles Lettres*. Edited by Harold F. Harding. 2 vols. Carbondale: Southern Illinois University Press, 1965.

Boileau-Despréaux, Nicolas. *Oeuvres complètes*. Edited by Antoine Adam. Paris: Editions Gallimard, 1966.

Borgerhoff, Elbert B. O. *The Freedom of French Classicism*. Princeton: Princeton University Press, 1950.

Bormann, Dennis R. "Some 'Common Sense' about Campbell, Hume, and Reid: The Extrinsic Evidence." *Quarterly Journal of Speech* 71 (1985): 395–421.

————. "George Campbell's *Cura Prima* on Eloquence—1758." *Quarterly Journal of Speech* 74 (1988): 35–51.

Bossuet, Jacques Bénigne. *Oeuvres oratoires*. Edited by J. Lebarq, Ch. Urbain and E. Levesque. Paris: Desclée de Bouvier et Cie, 1922.

Bouhours, Dominique. *Entretiens d'Ariste et d'Eugène*. Edited by René Radouant. 1671. Reprint. Paris: Bossard, 1920.

————. *La Manière de bien penser dans les ouvrages d'esprit*. Paris: Brunet, 1715. Reprint. Brighton: University of Sussex, 1971.

Boulvé, Léon. *De l'hellénisme chez Fénelon*. 1897. Reprint. Geneva: Slatkine, 1970.

Bourgoin, Auguste. *Les Maîtres de la critique au XVIIème siècle*. Paris: Garnier Frères, 1889.

Boze, Claude de. "Eloge de M. Despréaux." *Histoire de l'Académie Royale des Inscriptions et Belles Lettres* 3 (1746): 293–330

Brody, Jules. "Boileau and Longinus." Ph.D. diss., Columbia University, 1956.

————. *French Classicism: A Critical Miscellany*. Englewood Cliffs, NJ: Prentice-Hall, 1966.

Broglie, Emmanuel. *Fénelon à Cambrai d'après sa correspondance, 1699–1715*. Paris: Plon, 1884.

Buffon, Georges Louis Leclerc, Comte de. *Discours sur le style*. Paris: Société Générale de Librairie Catholique, 1882.

Burke, Edmund. *A Philosophical Enquiry into the Origin of Our Ideas of the Sublime and Beautiful*. Edited with an introduction by James T. Boulton. London: Routledge & Kegan Paul, 1958.

Campbell, George. *Lectures on Pulpit Eloquence*. London: John Bumpus, 1824.

————. *The Philosophy of Rhetoric*. New York: Harper & Brothers, 1859.

————. *The Philosophy of Rhetoric*. Edited by Lloyd F. Bitzer. Carbondale: Southern Illinois University Press, 1963; Revised, 1988.

Carcassonne, Ely. *Etat présent des travaux sur Fénelon*. Paris: Société d'Edition "Les Belles Lettres," 1939.

————. *Fénelon, l'homme et l'oeuvre*. Paris: Hatier-Boivin, 1946.

Cardy, Michael. "Crousaz and Hutcheson: Two Contributors to Aesthetic Ideas in the Early Eighteenth Century." *Humanities Association Review* 31 (1980): 29–44.

Carr, Thomas M., Jr. *Descartes and the Resilience of Rhetoric*. Carbondale: Southern Illinois University Press, 1990.

Carroll, Noel. "Hume's Standard of Taste." *Journal of Aesthetics and Art Criticism* 43 (1984): 181–94.

Cassirer, Ernst. *The Philosophy of the Enlightenment*. Translated by Fritz C. A. Koelin and James P. Pettegrove. Princeton: Princeton University Press, 1951.

Cherel, Albert. *Les Idées littéraires de Fénelon et la doctrine du «pur amour»*. Paris: Louvain, 1910.

————. *Fénelon au XVIIIème siècle en France, 1715–1820: Son prestige—son influence*. Paris: Librairie Hachette, 1917.

Chitnis, Anand C. *The Scottish Enlightenment: A Social History*. London: Croon Helm, 1976.

Clark, Alexander F. B. *Boileau and the French Classical Critics in England*. Paris: Edouard Champion, 1925.

Cohen, Herman. "Charles Rollin: Historian of Eloquence." *Western Speech* 22 (1958): 88–94.

Colloques Internationaux du Centre National de la Recherche Scientifique, no. 557. *Critique et création littéraires en France au XVIIe siècle*. Paris: Editions du Centre National de la Recherche Scientifique, 1977.

Crane, Ronald S., ed. *Critics and Criticism, Ancient and Modern*. Chicago: University of Chicago Press, 1952.

Crévier, Jean Baptiste. *Rhétorique française*. Paris, 1765. British and Continental Rhetoric and Elocution Microfilm.

Daiches, David, Peter Jones, and Jean Jones, eds. *A Hotbed of Genius: The Scottish Enlightenment, 1730–1790*. Edinburgh: Edinburgh University Press, 1986.

Davidson, Hugh. *Audience, Words, & Art: Studies in Seventeenth-Century French Rhetoric*. Columbus: Ohio State University Press, 1965.

Davis, James Herbert. *Fénelon*. Boston: Twayne Publishers, 1979.

Descartes, René. *Discours de la Méthode*. Edited by André Robinet. Paris: Larousse, 1972.

————. *Les Passions de l'âme*. Paris: Gallimard, 1988.

Dolph, Phil. "Taste and 'The Philosophy of Rhetoric.'" *Western Speech Journal* 32 (1968): 104–13.

Dubos, Jean-Baptiste. *Réflexions critiques sur la poésie et sur la peinture*. 3 vols. Utrecht: E. Neaulme, 1732–36.

Egger, E. *L'Hellénisme en France*. Paris: Didier, 1869.

Ehninger, Douglas W. "George Campbell and the Revolution in Inventional Theory." *Southern Speech Journal* 15 (1950): 270–76.

———. "Dominant Trends in English Rhetorical Thought, 1750–1800." *Southern Speech Journal* 18 (1952): 3–19.

Ehninger, Douglas W., and James Golden. "The Intrinsic Sources of Blair's Popularity." *Southern Speech Journal* 21 (1955): 12–30.

Fénelon, François de. *Dialogues sur l'éloquence*. Paris: Garnier Frères, 1866.

———. *Dialogues des morts*. Edited by J. Martin. 3d ed. Paris: Librairie Ch. Poussielque, 1899.

———. *Lettre à l'Académie*. Edited by Albert Cahen. Paris: Librairie Hachette, 1902.

———. *Lettre à l'Académie*. Edited by Ernesta Caldarini. Geneva: Librairie Droz, 1970.

———. *Correspondance de Fénelon*. Paris: Klincksieck, 1972.

Ferté, H. *Rollin, sa vie, ses oeuvres*. Paris: Hachette, 1902.

Finch, Robert. *The Sixth Sense: Individualism in French Poetry, 1686–1760*. Toronto: University of Toronto Press, 1966.

France, Peter. *Rhetoric and Truth in France: Descartes to Diderot*. New York: Oxford University Press, 1972.

Fumaroli, Marc. *L'Age de l'éloquence*. Geneva: Librairie Droz, 1980.

Gaudin, Albert C. *The Educational Views of Charles Rollin*. New York: Thesis Publishing Co., 1939.

Gerard, Alexander. *An Essay on Taste, Together with Observations Concerning the Imitative Nature of Poetry*. 3d ed. Introduction by Walter J. Hipple, Jr. 1780. Reprint. Gainesville, FL: Scholars' Facsimiles and Reprints, 1963.

Gibert, Balthasar. *Jugemens des savans sur les auteurs qui ont traité de la rhetorique*. 1725. Reprint. Hildesheim: Verlag, 1971.

———. *Observations adressées à M. Rollin, Ancien recteur et professeur royal, sur son Traité de la manière d'enseigner et d'étudier les belles lettres*. Paris: Françoise-Guillaume L'Hermite, 1727.

———. *La Rhétorique, ou les règles de l'éloquence*. Paris: Thiboust, 1730.

Golden, James L., and Edward P. J. Corbett. *The Rhetoric of Blair, Campbell, and Whately*. New York: Holt, 1968.

Golden, James, and Douglas Ehninger. "The Extrinsic Sources of Blair's Popularity." *Southern Speech Journal* 22 (1956): 16–32.

Goré, Jeanne-Lydie. *L'Itinéraire de Fénelon: Humanisme et spiritualité*. Paris: Presses Universitaires de France, 1957.

Grene, Marjorie. "Gerard's *Essay on Taste*." *Modern Philology* 41 (1943): 45–58.

Haight, Jeanne. *The Concept of Reason in French Classical Literature, 1635–1690*. Toronto: University of Toronto Press, 1982.

Harwood, John T., ed. *The Rhetorics of Thomas Hobbes and Bernard Lamy*. Carbondale: Southern Illinois University Press, 1986.

Havens, George Remington. *Age of Ideas*. New York: Holt, 1955.

Hazard, Paul. *La Pensée européenne au XVIIIème siècle*. 2 vols. Paris: Boivin, 1946.

Hipple, Walter John. *The Beautiful, the Sublime, and the Picturesque*. Carbondale: Southern Illinois University Press, 1957.

Holmes, John. *The Art of Rhetoric Made Easy or, the Elements of Oratory*. 2d ed. 2 vols. London: Hitch & Hawes, 1755.

Holub, Robert C. "The Rise of Aesthetics in the Eighteenth Century." *Comparative Literature Studies* 15 (1978): 271–83.

Home, Henry (Lord Kames). *Elements of Criticism*. 3 vols. 1762. Reprint. New York: Johnson Reprint Collection, 1967.

Hope, V. *Philosophers of the Scottish Enlightenment*. Edinburgh: The University Press, 1984.

Howell, Wilbur Samuel. *Fénelon's Dialogues on Eloquence*. Princeton: Princeton University Press, 1951.

———. *Eighteenth-Century British Logic and Rhetoric*. Princeton: Princeton University Press, 1971.

———. *Poetics, Rhetoric, and Logic: Studies in the Basic Disciplines of Criticism*. Ithaca, NY: Cornell University Press, 1975.

Hume, David. *An Enquiry Concerning Human Understanding*. Chicago: Open Court, 1949.

———. *Essays: Moral, Political, and Literary*. London: Oxford University Press, 1963.

———. *A Treatise of Human Nature*. 2d ed. Oxford: Clarendon Press, 1978.

———. *Essays: Moral, Political, and Literary*. Edited by Eugene F. Miller. Indianapolis, IN: Liberty Classics, 1984.

Hutcheson, Francis. *An Inquiry into the Original of our Ideas of Beauty and Virtue*. 4th ed. London: Midwinter, 1738. Reprint. Westmead: Gregg, 1969.

Irvine, James R. "James Beattie's Psychology of Taste." *Western Speech Journal* 34 (1970): 21–28.

Janet, Paul. *Fénelon: His Life and Works*. Port Washington, NY: Kennikat Press, 1914.

Jones, Peter. *Hume's Sentiments: Their Ciceronian and French Context*. Edinburgh: Edinburgh University Press, 1982.

———, ed. *The "Science of Man" in the Scottish Enlightenment*. Edinburgh: Edinburgh University Press, 1989.

Jourdain, Charles. *Histoire de l'Université de Paris au XVIIe et au XVIIIe siècle*. 2 vols. Paris: Firmin-Didot, 1888.

Kallich, Martin. "The Argument Against the Association of Ideas in Eighteenth-Century Aesthetics." *Modern Language Quarterly* 15 (1954): 125–36.

Keesey, Ray E. "John Lawson's *Lectures concerning Oratory*." *Speech Monographs* 20 (1955): 49–57.

Kivy, Peter. "Hume's Neighbor's Wife: An Essay on the Evolution of Hume's Aesthetics." *British Journal of Aesthetics* 23 (1983): 195–208.

Korsmeyer, Carolyn. "The Two Beauties: A Perspective on Hutcheson's Aesthetics." *Journal of Aesthetics and Art Criticism* 38 (1979): 145–51.

Ladborough, R. W. "Translation from the Ancients in Seventeenth-Century France." *Journal of the Warburg and Courtauld Institutes* 2 (1938): 85–104.

Laird, John. *Hume's Philosophy of Human Nature*. London: Methuen, 1932.

Lamy, Bernard. *De l'art de parler*. Paris: Pralard, 1676. British and Continental Rhetoric and Elocution Microfilm.

———. *La Rhétorique ou l'art de parler*. 4th ed. Amsterdam: Marrey, 1699.

Landolf, Gottfried. *Esthétique de Fénelon*. Zurich: Leeman, 1914.

Lang, Robert A. "Rhetoric at the University of Paris, 1550–1789." *Speech Monographs* 23 (1956): 216–28.

Lanson, M. Gustave. *Histoire de la littérature française*. Paris: Librairie Hachette, 1908.

Lawson, John. *Lectures concerning Oratory*. Edited by E. Neal Claussen and Karl R. Wallace. 1758. Reprint. Carbondale: Southern Illinois University Press, 1972.

Le Hir, Yves. *Rhétorique et stylistique de la Pléiade au Parnasse*. Paris: Presses Universitaires de France, 1960.

Lehmann, William C. *Henry Home, Lord Kames, and the Scottish Enlightenment*. The Hague: Nijhoff, 1971.

Litman, Théodore A. *Le Sublime en France: 1660–1714*. Paris: A. G. Nizet, 1971.

Little, Katharine Day. *François de Fénelon: Study of a Personality*. New York: Harper & Brothers, 1951.

Lombard, Alfred. *Fénelon et le retour à l'antique au XVIIIe Siècle*. Neuchâtel: Secrétariat de l'Université, 1954.

[Longinus?]. *On the Sublime*. Translated by W. Rhys Roberts. Cambridge: University Press, 1899.

———. *On the Sublime*. Translated by W. Hamilton Fyfe. Cambridge: Harvard University Press, 1927.

Macpherson, James, Esq., trans. *The Poems of Ossian*. Leipzig: Bernhard Tauchnitz, 1847.

Malherbe, François de. *Oeuvres poétiques de Malherbe*. Paris: Garnier Frères, 1917.

Manns, James. "The Scottish Influence on French Aesthetic Thought." *Journal of the History of Ideas* 49 (1988): 633–651.

Marshall, Keith. "France and the Scottish Press, 1700–1800." *Studies in Scottish Literature* 13 (1978): 1–14.

Massillon, Jean Baptiste. *Oeuvres complètes*. Paris: Guerin, 1865–1867.

Masson, Frédéric. *L'Académie française, 1629–1793*. Paris: Librairie Paul Ollendorf, 1912.

May, J. Lewis. *Fénelon, A Study*. London: Burnes, Oates, & Washbourne Limited, 1938.

Michael, Emily. "Francis Hutcheson on Aesthetic Perception and Aesthetic Pleasure." *British Journal of Aesthetics* 24 (1984): 241–55.

Michel, Alain. *La Parole et la beauté: Rhétorique et esthétique dans la tradition occidentale*. Paris: Les Belles Lettres, 1982.

Millar, J. H. *The Mid-Eighteenth Century*. Edinburgh: Blackwood, 1902.

Monk, Samuel. *The Sublime, A Study of Critical Theories of the Eighteenth Century in England*. Ann Arbor: University of Michigan Press, 1960.

Mornet, Daniel. *Histoire de la littérature française classique, 1660–1700*. 3d ed. Paris: Colin, 1947.

Munteano, Basil. "L'Abbé du Bos: Esthéticien de la persuasion passionnelle." *Revue de littérature comparée* 30 (1956): 318–49.

———. "Les Premisses rhetoriques du système de l'Abbé du Bos." *Rivista di Letterature Moderne e Comparate* 10 (1957): 5–30.

Mustoxidi, T. M. *Histoire de l'esthétique française, 1700–1900*. Paris: Champion, 1920.

Orcibal, J. "L'Influence de Fénelon dans les pays Anglo-Saxon au XVIIe Siècle," *Dix-Septième Siècle* 12–14 (1951–1952): 276–87.

Perelman, Chaim, and Lucie Olbrechts-Tyteca. *The New Rhetoric: A Treatise on Argumentation*. Translated by John Wilkinson and Purcell Weaver. Notre Dame: University of Notre Dame Press, 1969.

Perrault, Charles. *Parallèle des anciens et des modernes*. 4 vols. 1689–1697. Reprint. Munich: Eidos, 1964.

Pocock, Gordon. *Boileau and the Nature of Neo-Classicism*. Cambridge: Cambridge University Press, 1980.

Priestley, Joseph. *A Course of Lectures on Oratory and Criticism*. Edited by Vincent Bevilacqua and Richard Murphy. Carbondale: Southern Illinois University Press, 1965.

———. *A Course of Lectures on Oratory and Criticism, 1777*. Menston, England: The Scholar Press, Limited, 1968.

Proust, Jacques, ed. *Recherches nouvelles sur quelques écrivains des lumières*. Geneva: Droz, 1972.

Ramsay, Andrew Michael. *Histoire de la vie et des ouvrages de Messire François de Salignac de la Mothe-Fénelon, archevêque duc de Cambray*. Amsterdam: F. L'Honoré, 1729.

Rapin, René. *The Whole Critical Works of Mr. Rapin*. Translated by Basil Kennet, Mr. Rymer, and others. 2 vols. London: Walthoe, Wilkin, Birt, Ward, Wicksted, 1731.

Reid, Thomas, D.D. *Works*. Edited by William Hamilton. 8th ed. 2 vols. London: Longmans, 1895.

Rigualt, Hippolyte. *Histoire de la querelle des anciens et des modernes*. Paris: Librairie Hachette, 1856.

Robbins, David O. "The Aesthetics of Thomas Reid." *Journal of Aesthetics and Art Criticism* 1 (1942): 30–41.

Robertson, D. Maclaren. *A History of the French Academy, 1635–1910*. New York: Dillingham, 1935.

Rollin, Charles. *De la manière d'enseigner et d'étudier les Belles Lettres*. 4 vols. Lyon: Rusand, 1819.

Rubin, David Lee, and Mary B. McKinley, eds. *Convergences: Rhetoric and Poetic in Seventeenth-Century France*. Columbus: Ohio State University Press, 1989.

Saintsbury, George. *A History of Criticism and Literary Taste in Europe*. 3 vols. London: William Blackwood & Sons, 1900–1904.

Saisselin, Rémy G. *Taste in Eighteenth Century France*. Syracuse, NY: Syracuse University Press, 1965.

———. *The Rule of Reason and the Ruses of the Heart*. Cleveland, OH: Case Western Reserve University, 1970.

Sanders, E. K. *Fénelon: His Friends and His Enemies, 1651–1715*. London: Longmans, Green and Co., 1901.

Schmitz, Robert Morell. *Hugh Blair*. Morningside Heights, NY: King's Crown Press, 1948.

Sermain, Jean-Paul. *Rhétorique et roman au dix-huitième siècle*. Oxford: Alden Press, 1985.

Sher, Richard B. *Church and University in the Scottish Enlightenment*. Edinburgh: Edinburgh University Press, 1985.

Smith, Adam. *Essays on Philosophical Subjects*. London: Cadell and Davies, 1795. Reprint. Hildesheim: Verlag, 1982.

———. *Lectures on Rhetoric and Belles Lettres*. Edited by John M. Lothian. London: Nelson, 1963.

———. *The Theory of Moral Sentiments*. Edited by D. D. Raphael and A. L. Macfie. Oxford: Clarendon, 1976.

———. *Lectures on Rhetoric and Belles Lettres*. Edited by J. C. Bryce. Oxford: Clarendon, 1983.

Snyders, Georges. *La Pédagogie en France aux XVIIe et XVIIIe siècles.* Paris: Presses Universitaires de France, 1965.

Spence, Patricia R. "Sympathy and Propriety in Adam Smith's Rhetoric." *Quarterly Journal of Speech* 60 (1974): 92–99.

Stewart, Dugald. *Collected Works.* Edited by William Hamilton. 8 vols. Edinburgh: Constable, 1855.

Strosetzki, Christoph. *Rhétorique de la conversation.* Translated by Sabine Seubert. Paris: Papers on Seventeenth-Century Literature, 1984.

Swiggers, Pierre, ed. *Grammaire et méthode au XVIIe siècle.* Leuven: Peeters, 1984.

Tilley, Arthur. *The Decline of the Age of Louis XIV.* New York: Barnes and Noble, 1929.

Townsend, Dabney. "From Shaftesbury to Kant: The Development of the Concept of Aesthetic Experience." *Journal of the History of Ideas* 48 (1987): 287–305.

Varga, Aaron Kibédi. "La Rhétorique des passions et les genres." *Rhetorik* 6 (1989): 67–83.

Varillon, François. *Fénelon et le pur amour.* Paris: Editions de Seuil, 1957.

Vickers, Brian. *In Defence of Rhetoric.* Oxford: Clarendon Press, 1988.

Vickers, Brian, and Nancy S. Struever. *Rhetoric and the Pursuit of Truth: Language Change in the Seventeenth and Eighteenth Centuries.* Los Angeles: Clark Memorial Library, 1985.

Vincent, Leon H. *The French Academy.* New York: Houghton, Mifflin and Co., 1901.

Voitle, Robert. *The Third Earl of Shaftesbury, 1671–1713.* Baton Rouge: Louisiana State University Press, 1984.

Warnick, Barbara. "Fénelon's Recommendations to the French Academy Concerning Rhetoric." *Communication Monographs* 45 (1978): 75–84.

———. "Rhetoric and the *Encyclopédie*." *Central States Speech Journal* 29 (1978): 283–92.

———. "The Old Rhetoric vs. the New Rhetoric: The Quarrel between the Ancients and the Moderns." *Communication Monographs* 49 (1982): 263–76.

———. "Charles Rollin's *Traité* and the Rhetorical Theories of Smith, Campbell, and Blair." *Rhetorica* 3 (1985): 45–65.

———. "The Most Significant Passage in Hugh Blair's *Lectures on Rhetoric and Belles Lettres*." *Rhetoric Society Quarterly* 17 (1987): 301–04.

———, ed. and trans. *Fénelon's Letter to the French Academy.* Lanham, MD: University Press of America, 1984.

Wieand, Jeffrey. "Hume's Two Standards of Taste." *The Philosophical Quarterly* 34 (1984): 129–42.

White, Julian Eugene, Jr. *Nicolas Boileau*. New York: Twayne Publishers, 1969.

Index

abstraction, 86

Addison, Joseph, 60

admiration, 119–120; as a passion, 21, 88

adresse, 29–30, 45

aesthetics: empiricist, 122–27; origins of taste in, 109–10; the Sublime, 81

Alembert, Jean Le Rond d', 112

allegory, 120

animal spirits, 23, 31, 123

antithesis, 120

appropriateness, 38, 83, 92, 130. *See also* Propriety

Aristotle, 17, 18, 61; *Rhetoric,* 51; *Topics,* 27

Arnauld, Antoine, 31; *La Logique, ou l'art de penser,* 42. *See also* Nicole, Pierre; Port Royalism

arrangement, 71, 47; in Adam Smith's lectures, 59; proportion in, 54–55. *See also* Disposition

association: as a means of rhetorical appeal, 31; psychological theory of, 7, 9, 23, 58, 104, 130–31. *See also* psychology, associationist

audience: adaptation to, 61, 71

Augustine, St., 51, 54, 39

Bacon, Francis, 9

Balzac, Jean-Louis Guez de, 15

barbarism, 64

Beattie, James, 107, 116

beauty: perception of, 116–17

belletrism: features of, 2–3, 22; French, 6–10, 15; its interest in aesthetics, 45; Scottish, 133

belletrists: as model critics, 3–6

Bevilacqua, Vincent, 84–85, 107, 113; "Lord Kames's Theory of Rhetoric," 13; "Philosophical Assumptions Underlying Hugh Blair's *Lectures on Rhetoric and Belles Lettres,*" 14; "Philosophical Origins of George Campbell's *Philosophy of Rhetoric,*" 13; "The Rhetorical Theory of Henry Home, Lord Kames," 12

bienséance, 15, 47–49, 71, 75; characteristics of, 39; defined, 32; Fénelon's conception of, 50–57. *See also* Propriety

Bitzer, Lloyd, 11

Bizzell, Patricia, 90

Blair, Hugh, 34, 96–97, 128, 130; "Critical Dissertation on the Poems of Ossian," 70; disparagement of the topics, 20; knowledge of French language, 15; *Lectures on Rhetoric and Belles Lettres,* 2–4, 90, 131–35; reliance on Dubos, 122–23; reliance on em-

171

3 5282 00428 1740